An Analysis of

David J. Teece's

Dynamic Capabilities and Strategic Management: Organizing for Innovation and Growth

Veselina Stoyanova

Published by Macat International Ltd
24:13 Coda Centre, 189 Munster Road, London SW6 6AW

Distributed exclusively by Routledge
2 Park Square, Milton Park, Abingdon, Oxon OX14 4RN
711 Third Avenue, New York, NY 10017, USA

Routledge is an imprint of the Taylor & Francis Group, an informa business

www.macat.com
info@macat.com

Cataloguing in Publication Data
A catalogue record for this book is available from the British Library.
Library of Congress Cataloguing-in-Publication Data is available upon request.
Cover illustration: David Newton

ISBN 978-1-912453-49-8 (hardback)
ISBN 978-1-912453-04-7 (paperback)
ISBN 978-1-912453-19-1 (e-book)

Notice
The information in this book is designed to orientate readers of the work under analysis,
to elucidate and contextualise its key ideas and themes, and to aid in the development
of critical thinking skills. It is not meant to be used, nor should it be used, as a
substitute for original thinking or in place of original writing or research. References and
notes are provided for informational purposes and their presence does not constitute
endorsement of the information or opinions therein. This book is presented solely for
educational purposes. It is sold on the understanding that the publisher is not engaged
to provide any scholarly advice. The publisher has made every effort to ensure that
this book is accurate and up-to-date, but makes no warranties or representations with
regard to the completeness or reliability of the information it contains. The information
and the opinions provided herein are not guaranteed or warranted to produce particular
results and may not be suitable for students of every ability. The publisher shall not be
liable for any loss, damage or disruption arising from any errors or omissions, or from
the use of this book, including, but not limited to, special, incidental, consequential or
other damages caused, or alleged to have been caused, directly or indirectly, by the
information contained within.

Printed and bound by CPI Group (UK) Ltd, Croydon, CR0 4YY

CONTENTS

THE MACAT LIBRARY

The Macat Library is a series of unique academic explorations of seminal works in the humanities and social sciences – books and papers that have had a significant and widely recognised impact on their disciplines. It has been created to serve as much more than just a summary of what lies between the covers of a great book. It illuminates and explores the influences on, ideas of, and impact of that book. Our goal is to offer a learning resource that encourages critical thinking and fosters a better, deeper understanding of important ideas.

Each publication is divided into three Sections: Influences, Ideas, and Impact. Each Section has four Modules. These explore every important facet of the work, and the responses to it.

This Section-Module structure makes a Macat Library book easy to use, but it has another important feature. Because each Macat book is written to the same format, it is possible (and encouraged!) to cross-reference multiple Macat books along the same lines of inquiry or research. This allows the reader to open up interesting interdisciplinary pathways.

To further aid your reading, lists of glossary terms and people mentioned are included at the end of this book (these are indicated by an asterisk [*] throughout) – as well as a list of works cited.

Macat has worked with the University of Cambridge to identify the elements of critical thinking and understand the ways in which six different skills combine to enable effective thinking.
Three allow us to fully understand a problem; three more give us the tools to solve it. Together, these six skills make up the **PACIER** model of critical thinking. They are:

ANALYSIS – understanding how an argument is built
EVALUATION – exploring the strengths and weaknesses of an argument
INTERPRETATION – understanding issues of meaning

CREATIVE THINKING – coming up with new ideas and fresh connections
PROBLEM-SOLVING – producing strong solutions
REASONING – creating strong arguments

To find out more, visit **WWW.MACAT.COM.**

CRITICAL THINKING AND *DYNAMIC CAPABILITIES AND STRATEGIC MANAGEMENT*

Primary critical thinking skill: INTERPRETATION
Secondary critical thinking skill: REASONING

David Teece's aim is to explore and clarify how companies can sustain their market position and performance in rapidly changing environments. He develops the dynamic capability framework (sensing, seizing and reconfiguring activities) to address these company competences.

Nevertheless, Teece does not develop his theoretical assumptions and the dynamic capability framework in isolation from previous research. On the contrary, the work is built through a process of critical interpretation and reasoning.

Teece pays substantial attention to interpreting ideas and comparing conventional strategy models and theories such as Porter's Five Forces and the resource-based view of the firm. Throughout the book, the author provides a good number of example companies facing rapid changes in their industry, which assists in producing well-structured and persuasive arguments.

ABOUT THE AUTHOR OF THE ORIGINAL WORK

David Teece was born in New Zealand in 1948. He is currently a Professor in Global Business at the Haas School of Business at the University of California, Berkeley. Teece is an influential scholar on matters of industrial organization, technological change, and innovation. He is mostly known for coining the concept "dynamic capability" and has been recognized by Accenture as one of the world's top 50 business intellectuals.

ABOUT THE AUTHOR OF THE ANALYSIS

Veselina Stoyanova is an Assistant Professor in Strategy at the Department of Strategy and Organisation in Strathclyde Business School. She holds a PhD in Management (Strategy and International Business focus) from the University of Edinburgh, and her research interests center on the process of dynamic capability development, issues of organizational change, strategic development and adaptation during times of uncertainty and complexity.

Dr Stoyanova has also worked as a consultant at Kempen Capital Management and for the Ministry of Economy and Energy of the Republic of Bulgaria.

ABOUT MACAT

GREAT WORKS FOR CRITICAL THINKING

Macat is focused on making the ideas of the world's great thinkers accessible and comprehensible to everybody, everywhere, in ways that promote the development of enhanced critical thinking skills.

It works with leading academics from the world's top universities to produce new analyses that focus on the ideas and the impact of the most influential works ever written across a wide variety of academic disciplines. Each of the works that sit at the heart of its growing library is an enduring example of great thinking. But by setting them in context – and looking at the influences that shaped their authors, as well as the responses they provoked – Macat encourages readers to look at these classics and game-changers with fresh eyes. Readers learn to think, engage and challenge their ideas, rather than simply accepting them.

'Macat offers an amazing first-of-its-kind tool for interdisciplinary learning and research. Its focus on works that transformed their disciplines and its rigorous approach, drawing on the world's leading experts and educational institutions, opens up a world-class education to anyone.'

Andreas Schleicher,
Director for Education and Skills, Organisation for Economic
Co-operation and Development

'Macat is taking on some of the major challenges in university education ... They have drawn together a strong team of active academics who are producing teaching materials that are novel in the breadth of their approach.'

Prof Lord Broers,
former Vice-Chancellor of the University of Cambridge

'The Macat vision is exceptionally exciting. It focuses upon new modes of learning which analyse and explain seminal texts which have profoundly influenced world thinking and so social and economic development. It promotes the kind of critical thinking which is essential for any society and economy. This is the learning of the future.'

Rt Hon Charles Clarke, former UK Secretary of State for Education

'The Macat analyses provide immediate access to the critical conversation surrounding the books that have shaped their respective discipline, which will make them an invaluable resource to all of those, students and teachers, working in the field.'

Professor William Tronzo, University of California at San Diego

WAYS IN TO THE TEXT

KEY POINTS

- David Teece is best known for coining the term *dynamic capability** and developing its attendant theory.

- *Dynamic Capabilities and Strategic Management* examines how the firm can sustain competitive advantages, especially in times of change and uncertainty.

- Teece breaks with conventional models to argue that the essence of strategy formulation is creating business models and technologies that can sustain competitive advantages.

Who is David J. Teece?

David John Teece was born on September 2, 1948, in Blenheim, New Zealand, and is now a researcher and professor of Global Business at University of California, Berkley.

The son of an entrepreneur, Teece spent his early years in New Zealand, where he received Bachelor's and Master's degrees in communications. Later he moved to the United States, where he attended the Wharton School of the University of Pennsylvania, and pursued a PhD in economics specializing in industrial economics. Growing up in a family with older brothers, he was exposed from an early age to their economics textbooks. An important factor in Teece's intellectual growth was the influence of his supervisor at the

Wharton School, Edwin Mansfield,* who encouraged Teece to follow his interest in technology and technology transfer.

Interested in economics—examining the business environment and competition—but also in organizational innovation, Teece drew upon both disciplines to create what is now known as the "dynamic capabilities" theory. The emergence of Teece's concept of dynamic capability came at a time when scholarly dialogue was still centered around traditional economic assumptions that tended to explain only in part how companies manage to generate wealth for both shareholders and stakeholders. While traditional industrial economics research focuses on the industry specifications to suggest that a company's competitiveness would often depend on its market positioning within its industry, Teece calls for a better examination of the company's specific characteristics.

To date, he has authored 30 books and 200 research papers. He is also a co-editor of the Palgrave *Encyclopedia of Strategic Management*.[1]

What does *Dynamic Capabilities and Strategic Management* say?

Dynamic Capabilities was written in Berkeley, California in 2009. The book can be perceived as the product of a number of works authored or co-authored by Teece over the preceding 20 years, which have become, collectively, some of the most cited works in business and economics worldwide. The book's fundamental idea comes from a 1990 working paper in which Teece, together with Gary Pisano* and Amy Shuen,* coined the term "dynamic capability." This paper was subsequently published in *Strategic Management Journal* and received the Strategic Management Society's best paper award in 2003.

In *Dynamic Capabilities,* Teece addresses the core question of how a company can create and sustain a competitive advantage in changing environments and against extensive market competition. To answer this question, Teece explores how a company's management can notice business opportunities in the marketplace, make decisions and take action to seize those opportunities, and still be able to adapt to rapid changes in order to generate economic surpluses.

There are four main themes in the book. The first is concerned with the role and the importance of dynamic capabilities theory in the study of strategic management and organizational performance. The second theme highlights the practical and theoretical contributions of entrepreneurs, leaders, and managers not only inside the company but also externally in economic systems. In this regard, Teece views managers and entrepreneurs as important in their ability to identify and capture new business opportunities, to orchestrate organizational assets and to create newer and more effective business models and organizational forms. Third, he argues that unbiased decision-making needs to be achieved through the design of effective organizational structures and incentive programs. The fourth theme sets out his hope that the dynamic capabilities framework can help develop a theory of strategy that regards strategic processes as evolutionary. These themes emerge in Teece's discussion of strategic management concepts as they relate to the development of dynamic capabilities framework.

According to Teece, the first process in the dynamic capabilities framework—*sensing*—includes a number of microfoundations* such as: to direct internal research and development and select new technologies through processes; to tap supplier and complementary innovation; to harness developments in exogenous* science and technology; and to identify target market segments, allowing for changes in customers' needs. The second process in the framework—*seizing opportunities*—involves elements such as the selection of product architectures and business models, the setting of enterprise boundaries, the management process of complements and business platforms and the ability to avoid biases, delusion, deception, and hubris. The third process in the framework is *managing threats* and *reconfiguration* of activities. Teece argues that this can be achieved by decentralization and decomposition of the firm's business structure, co-specialization, but also through knowledge management and good governance structure, which assist the flow of technology.

Beyond the theoretical contributions that they present, Teece's ideas are a useful analytical tool to business practitioners and consultants in large multinational companies undertaking organizational changes affecting their business ecosystems. According to the Web of Knowledge and Google Scholar, *Dynamic Capabilities* remains not only Teece's most cited work but also the most cited work on dynamic capabilities. David Teece has currently been cited more than 100,000 times, according to Google.[2]

Why does *Dynamic Capabilities and Strategic Management* matter?

Dynamic Capabilities can be characterized as a "game-changer" in the management and strategy field, especially in the study of multinational enterprise performance. It builds upon a number of disciplines such as strategy, decision-making, organizational science, management and economics, as well as theories such as transaction-cost economics,* the resource-based theory of the firm and evolutionary economics.* By combining management theories with social science disciplines, it provides insights for both academics and practitioners who are looking for an understanding of competition and wealth creation. Teece's work also stands out for its analysis of the challenges that multinational companies (MNCs)* tend to face in the contemporary knowledge-based economy, especially in terms of sustaining their competitive advantages.

The text is original both in its structure and its theoretical development. Its considerable impact in the field of strategy and management science can be attributed to the central contribution of Teece's work, his development of the dynamic capabilities framework, which helps to explain how companies can change and adapt during turbulent times to sustain their competitive advantages. The three processes identified by Teece—sensing, seizing and reconfiguring—have become a frequently used analytical framework for researchers interested in the study of organizational change.

Teece's dynamic capabilities view breaks with previously conventional models and theories such as Michael Porter's Five Forces model, and highlights the shortcomings of other theoretical developments such as Edith Penrose's* resource-based view, to argue that the essence of strategy formulation is not "coping with competition," as Porter states, but rather the creation of business models and technologies that can sustain competitive advantages.[3]

In regards to Porter's framework, Teece argues that it tends to give little attention to the firm itself and its capabilities. After Porter's model, Penrose's resource-based* theory of the firm offers another way of escaping the economic equilibrium trap. According to Penrose, a company can increase its profits and performance by possessing scarce, desirable (to customers) and hard-to-imitate products and services. In *Dynamic Capabilities*, Teece shares some of Penrose's ideas, in particular her argument that managers' and entrepreneurs' competences should be viewed as valuable resources that can help the company achieve a competitive position in the marketplace. However, he criticizes the static approach of her model as failing to explain how companies can sustain their resources in the future, in cases of sudden change.

NOTES

1   Teece, DJ. (2018) *The Scholar Entrepreneur*, available at http://davidjteece. com/. Accessed February 24th 2018.

2   Tom, P. (2012) *Profs. David Teece and Ross Levine Achieve 100K Citations*, available at http://newsroom.haas.berkeley.edu/profs-david-teece-and-ross-levine-achieve-100k-citations/. Accessed January 7th 2018.

3   Teece D.J, Pisano, G, Shuen, A. 1997. Dynamic capabilities and strategic management. *Strategic Management Journal* 18(7): 509–533.

SECTION 1
INFLUENCES

MODULE 1
THE AUTHOR AND THE
HISTORICAL CONTEXT

KEY POINTS

- Teece explores the question of how a company can create and sustain competitive advantage in changing environments.

- Teece was influenced by Edwin Mansfield of the Wharton School of Business.

- Teece's core ideas were developed in 1993 during a period of rapid globalization, increased market competition and socio-political changes.

Why Read This Text?

David J. Teece's *Dynamic Capabilities and Strategic Management* offers a deep understanding of the literature on dynamic capabilities by drawing on studies of economic theory and organizations, as well as innovation. As its title suggests, the main topic of the book is the role of dynamic capabilities in strategic processes for achieving a sustainable business performance.

In this work, Teece addresses the core question of how a company can create and sustain a competitive advantage in changing environments and against extensive market competition. Teece argues that conventional elements such as possessing rare tangible and intangible resources, inventory, high product or process quality may be necessary for business success and competitiveness, but they are not sufficient. He suggests that the real sources of a competitive advantage, which can be sustained even in changing environments, are dynamic capabilities, which integrate, build and reconfigure internal and

> ❝ I had the good fortune of having a brother who was studying economics and he brought home a copy of Lee Bach's introductory textbook (Bach, 1954). I picked it up and started reading it and there were ideas that I found very interesting and so I told myself that this was the subject that I wanted to study. ❞
>
> Mie Augier, *The Evolving Dynamics of Organizational Capabilities: An Interview with David J. Teece*

external competencies. Thus, the dynamic capability view extends the static nature of the resource-based view of the firm.

The book, and more specifically Teece's dynamic capability framework, is a useful analytical tool for students and academics exploring how a company's management can notice business opportunities in the marketplace, make decisions and take action to seize those opportunities, and still be able to adapt to rapid changes in order to generate economic surpluses.

Author's Life

Teece is a researcher and professor of Global Business and a director of the Centre for Global Strategy and Governance at University of California. He was born on 2nd of September 1948 in Blenheim, New Zealand, and to date has authored more than 150 books and articles, as well as advising the governments of a number of countries, among them Australia, the United Kingdom, the United States and New Zealand. The son of an entrepreneur, he spent his early years in New Zealand, where he received Bachelor's and Master's degrees in communications.

Teece's educational and family background had a significant influence on his specific interests and development as a researcher. Growing up in a family with older brothers, he was exposed from an early age to their economics textbooks. His passionate interest in the field of economics led to his acceptance as a doctoral student at the University of Pennsylvania's Wharton School of Business and his subsequent development as a well-known researcher. At Wharton, Teece studied Ph.D. in economics with a specialization in industrial economics. An important factor in Teece's intellectual growth was the influence of his doctoral supervisor, Edwin Mansfield, who inspired Teece's interest in technology and technology transfer.

Author's Background

The core ideas discussed in Teece's *Dynamic Capabilities* were developed during a period when organizational, technological and socio-political changes were taking place both locally and globally. As companies became international and market competition increased, the assumptions of conventional industrial economics needed to be revised and adapted. Teece's work analyses companies' organizational adaptation and development processes in order to shed light on new phenomena, as well as revisiting earlier theories and their conceptual underpinnings.

His attempts to explain how companies can improve their performance, and which factors influence a company's competences, first came to widespread attention within the research community in 1994 with the publication of the co-authored journal article "The Dynamic Capabilities of Firms,"[1] where Teece argued that there are some cases where neither economies of scale* nor economies of scope* determine the scope and the scale of a business enterprise, this being instead determined by contractual access to scale-based facilities.*

Both economic and political circumstances can be recognized as influential factors in the emergence of Teece's conceptual framework. In economic terms, his work came at a time when investment in high technology was growing significantly, and outsourcing was becoming a common strategy for companies seeking economies of scope in emerging market countries, as these countries' governments increasingly opened their internal markets to international businesses.

NOTES

1   David J. Teece and Gary Pisano, "The Dynamic Capabilities of Firms: An Introduction," *Industrial and Corporate Change* 3, no. 3 (1994): 537–56.

MODULE 2
ACADEMIC CONTEXT

KEY POINTS

* Teece's theories were informed by his interests in business environments and organizational innovation.
* He addresses gaps in the earlier work of Michael Porter and Edith Penrose.
* Teece argues that contractual theory cannot fully explain how a company attains sustainable advantage.

The Work in its Context

Prior to the landmark *Dynamic Capabilities and Strategic Management*, David J. Teece was interested in both economics—examining the business environment and competition—but also in organizational innovation. Teece drew upon both disciplines to create what is now known as the dynamic capabilities theory.

The emergence of Teece's concept of dynamic capability came at a time when scholarly dialogue was still centered on traditional economic assumptions that tended to explain only in part how companies manage to generate wealth for both shareholders and stakeholders. While traditional industrial economics research focuses on the industry specifications to suggest that a company's competitiveness would often depend on its market positioning within its industry, Teece called for a better examination of the company's specific characteristics.

As companies became international, and market competition increased, the assumptions of conventional industrial economics needed to be revised and adapted. Teece's work analyses companies' organizational adaptation and development processes in order to shed

> 66 Teece is one of the founding fathers of strategic management as we know it today; he pioneered research on both the resource based approach and especially dynamic capabilities, thereby helping to establish the competence based perspective on economic organization. 99
>
> Mie Augier, *The Evolving Dynamics of Organizational Capabilities: An Interview with David J. Teece*

light on new phenomena as well as to revisit earlier theories and their conceptual underpinnings. Teece's work extends industrial economics theories by directing the attention of management scholarship towards a closer study of a firm's intangible resources and capabilities, which he regards as central for sustainable business performance and competitiveness.

Overview of the Field

Before the emergence of Teece's theory, the strategy field was dominated by industrial economics based theories. Sustainable business performance was explained by the use of economic analysis and the economic theory of the firm (e.g., Porter's Five Forces) in which firms achieve sustainability by escaping economic equilibrium. After Porter's model, Penrose's resource-based theory of the firm offers another way of escaping the economic equilibrium trap. According to Edith Penrose, a company can increase its profits and performance by possessing scarce, desirable (to customers) and hard-to-imitate products and services.

Teece's core enquiry in the book and his dynamic capabilities theory addresses some of the gaps in earlier theories of the firm such as behavioral theory of the firm, transaction cost theory and evolutionary theories of the firm and strategy. In *Dynamic Capabilities*,

Teece uses some of Penrose's ideas, in particular her argument that managers' and entrepreneurs' competences should be viewed as valuable resources that can help the company achieve a competitive position in the marketplace. However, he criticizes the static approach of her model as failing to explain how companies can sustain their resources in the future, in cases of sudden change.

Academic Influences

An important factor in Teece's intellectual growth was the influence of his supervisor at the Wharton School, Edwin Mansfield, who encouraged him to follow his passion for studying technology and technology transfer issues. One of his mentors in University of Pennsylvania was also the Nobel laureate Oliver Williamson,* known for his work on transaction cost theories. Teece's close interaction with Oliver Williamson and Edwin Mansfield inspired his deep interest and critical study of factors influencing company performance. In contrast to contractual theorists such as Williamson, known for their work on transaction cost economics along with proponents of Porter's industrial analysis, Teece argues that contractual theorists tend to provide significant insight into the macro-level factors influencing a company's performance, but they do not go deep enough to identify the real components of a company's sustainable advantages.

Soon after his graduation from Wharton, Teece took up a teaching and research fellowship at Stanford University and later moved on to the University of California, Berkeley. In these respected institutions, Teece found himself among highly ranked and talented researchers in the field of organizational science and business strategy. His discussions with members of these knowledge communities, such as Harbir Singh*and Sidney Winter,* inspired his further thinking on fundamental questions of corporate competitiveness and performance in the strategic management field.

MODULE 3
THE PROBLEM

KEY POINTS

- The core research question in the strategic management field is how a firm can sustain their competitiveness and outperform competition.

- Porter's Five Forces model, game theoretical* approach and the resource-based view were the three major views prior to Teece's work.

- Teece claims that a dynamic capabilities framework is essential in the context of a hypercompetitive environment.*

Core Question

Similar to other researchers in the field of business strategy, David Teece shared an interest in exploring how a firm can sustain their competitiveness and outperform competition. In his work *Dynamic Capabilities and Strategic Management,* Teece seeks explanations on how a company can create and sustain a competitive advantage in changing environments and against extensive market competition. Earlier industrial economics informed theories of the firm, such as Michael Porter's Five Forces model, examine competitiveness by analyzing a company's position in the industry it operates and the ability to escape economic equilibrium. Other theoretical perspectives such as Penrose's resource based view of the firm explore sustainable competitive advantage by looking at the resources that the company possesses.

In contrast to earlier theorizations on the questions, Teece emphasizes the importance of focusing on how a company's management can notice business opportunities in the marketplace,

> ** 66 ** The dominant paradigm in the field during the 1980s was the competitive forces approach developed by Porter (1980). This approach, rooted in the structure–conduct–performance paradigm of industrial organization (Mason, 1949; Bain, 1959), emphasizes the actions a firm can take to create defensible positions against competitive forces. ** 99 **
>
> David Teece, Gary Pisano, and Amy Shuen, *Dynamic Capabilities and Strategic Management*

make decisions and take action to seize those opportunities, and still be able to adapt to rapid changes in order to generate economic surpluses. This core question is significant for the understanding of how competitive advantages are sustained by the firm, especially in times of change. Teece's integrated approach allows him to develop a robust framework containing richly detailed descriptions of a company's factors and patterns.

The Participants

Before the emergence of the dynamic capability view, the strategic management field was dominated by industrial organization scholars such as Michael Porter, who focused on examining the structure of the market and the nature of the competition in different industries, as well as the game theoretical approach to strategic management and the resource- based perspective.

Porter has been excellent in translating industrial organization and marketing ideas into useful managerial framework for doing industry analysis such as Porter's Five Forces model, which looks at the strengths of five factors that affect competition of a business. The Five Forces are (1) the threat of new entrants in an industry, (2) the threat of substitutes, (3) the bargaining power of customers, (4) the bargaining power of suppliers, and (5) the rivalry in a given industry. The higher the strengths of the Five Forces, the less likely it is for a firm to succeed in a given industry.

The game theoretical approach to strategic management argues that firms could gain competitive advantage by a series of strategic moves and the resource based perspective. The resource-based view argues that the firm can be viewed as a collection of resources. It is believed that Edith Penrose was the precursor of the theory. However, at the time she was more interested in exploring the growth of the firm rather than its strategy. In fact, it was Teece who first applied Penrose's ideas to strategic management. Jay Barney* formalized the theory further in 1991 by discussing company's resources as both tangible and intangible and also introducing the VRIN framework, examining firm resources as valuable, rare, imitable and non-substitutable. According to the resource-based view, a firm which possesses rare, valuable, non-imitable and non-substitutable resources would have a sustainable competitive advantage.[1]

The Contemporary Debate

David Teece's work does not oppose these traditional views, but in addition to these three major traditions he suggested a perspective which helps to study the kind of capabilities that a firm must acquire to establish competitive advantage in industries with rapid technological change. According to Teece, integrating economic theories with strategic management could address both theoretical and practical issues related to organizational design and firm boundaries.

One of the leading theories at that time, triggering significant interest and further streams of research, was Edith Penrose's theory of the growth of the firm, establishing the foundations for Barney's 1991 resource based view of the firm, which views a company's tangible and intangible resources as a source of competitive advantage.

Teece emphasizes some similarities between earlier theorizations of resource based view and the dynamic theory of the firm, especially regarding the importance of intangible resources for company prosperity. However, after exploring Penrose's intellectual work in depth, Teece concluded that her framework does not address the changing environment in which companies usually operate. She considers learning only as an opportunity for better performance; he prefers to view it as a necessary resource for a company's prosperity. He also noticed that her theory was lacking a discussion on organizational design, as it relates to incentive programs and modes of decision-making, though she recognizes the importance of the human resource element in every firm. In Teece's view, entrepreneurial activities have a tight relationship with managerial activities, as both are essential for the development of dynamic capabilities in multinational companies (MNCs).*

Teece claims that rather than relying on the resource-based view's static framework, a dynamic capabilities framework is essential in the context of a hypercompetitive environment.

NOTES

1   Mie-Sophia Augier, *The Evolving Dynamics of Organizational Capabilities: An Interview with David J. Teece*. København. 2004:36.

MODULE 4
THE AUTHOR'S CONTRIBUTION

KEY POINTS

- Teece tries to explain how companies sustain competitive advantages over time and how they adapt to organizational change processes.

- He directs attention towards the decision-making and learning processes.

- He contributes to the strategic field, explaining that companies' sustained competitive advantage originates in part from their capacity to renew competences.

Author's Aims

In developing dynamic capabilities theory, David J. Teece sought to explain how companies sustain competitive advantages over time, and how they adapt to organizational change processes such as technological innovations. He integrated research findings and knowledge from the fields of strategy, industrial economics, business history, innovation and organizational science, producing a framework that he hoped would become a useful tool for both practitioners and researchers. Moreover, he intended the dynamic capabilities framework to advance the neo–Schumpeterian theory* of the firm and of organizational decision-making, as well as the resource-based view of the firm.

Teece's framework goes beyond traditional thinking in its analysis of companies' competitive advantages: it not only explains the processes and patterns necessary for strong positioning in the marketplace, but also explores companies' decision-making processes. Moreover, it also aims to integrate ideas of adaptation, reconfiguration,

> ❝ The dynamic capabilities framework analyzes the sources and methods of wealth creation and capture by private enterprise firms operating in environments of rapid technological change. ❞
>
> David Teece, Gary Pisano and Amy Shuen, *Dynamic Capabilities and Strategic Management*

integration and flexibility. The work starts with Teece's theorization on the micro-foundations of dynamic capabilities, and then explains the fundamental role of the manager in the process of developing these capabilities. It explores in detail the foundations of dynamic capabilities and their relationship with a company's business resources, competences and Edith Penrose's framework. Teece ends his work with an explanation of the role of the dynamic capabilities framework within the context of multinational companies (MNCs), especially in times of rapid change.

Approach

In the strategic management field, there are a number of models, developed to explain how a firm can develop competitive advantage (e.g. Michael Porter's 1980s competitive forces model; the resource-based view of the firm). In contrast to earlier explanations, Teece argues that traditional prerequisites for business success such as owning tangible assets, achieving high service/product quality, controlling costs, and inventory optimization are necessary yet not sufficient for sustaining performance over the long run of organizational life. Teece proposes that organizational success depends on a firm's ability to refresh its resource base. Thus, the real source of sustainable firm competitiveness is in the 'dynamic capabilities' that an organization possesses when the environment changes.

Instead of simply focusing on analyzing the resources through the dynamic capability view, Teece directs scholarly and managerial attention towards the decision-making and learning processes, which support the development of core competences and organizational capabilities. In Teece's view, firms develop dynamic capabilities by engaging in learning activities such as market research, collection of competitive intelligence, knowledge about customers' preferences, benchmarking, research and development activities. The author sees competition not as an obstacle for firm success but as a contributor to organizational learning. According to Teece, companies find out how well they are performing in the marketplace in comparison with their competitors.

Contribution in Context

Teece's ideas and academic contributions are believed to be more interdisciplinary in comparison with those of fellow scholars. His contributions build on ideas from transaction cost theory, evolutionary economics, covering different levels of the organization. Teece's interest in explaining the basis of a company's competitiveness and sustainable performance led him to an in-depth study of the earlier views of the resource-based theory, emphasizing that accumulating valuable technological assets in a high technology industry can support a significant competitive advantage.

However, besides the importance of organizational resources, Teece argues that winners in the global marketplace will be companies that demonstrate timely responsiveness and rapid flexible innovation, at the same time possessing a management capability to coordinate and redeploy internal and external competences effectively. According to Teece, a firm can possess a large stock of valuable assets but still not have useful capabilities, which will sustain its competitiveness. In order to sustain competitive advantage, companies would need not only to possess valuable resources and unique competences as the earlier resource-based view of the firm suggests, but also to have the capacity to renew competences in line with the changing business environment. He coined the term 'dynamic capabilities' to emphasize these dynamics which were not at the center of academic research or thinking in the strategy field at the time.

SECTION 2
IDEAS

MODULE 5
MAIN IDEAS

KEY POINTS

- Teece's main themes are the importance and significance of dynamic capability theory, its contributions to practice for strategists and entrepreneurs, and its evolutionary nature.

- Dynamic capabilities have three main functions: sensing opportunities and threats, seizing opportunities, and reconfiguring organizational assets and structures to adapt to change.

- Teece's ideas are easy to follow and understand by business practitioners as well as academics in the strategy field.

Key Themes

In *Dynamic Capabilities and Strategic Management*, David J. Teece develops four main themes: the nature of dynamic capabilities and their microfoundations,[1] the entrepreneurial role of the manager in orchestrating organization assets[2] and creating new business models,[3] discussion of the intellectual roots of the dynamic capability framework, and its relationship to theories of the firm.[4]

These themes emerge in Teece's discussion of strategic management concepts as they relate to the dynamic capabilities framework; he discusses each one in in great detail, rigorously and consistently in line with his stated intent.

The first is concerned with the role and the importance of dynamic capabilities theory in the study of strategic management and organizational performance. It is mainly discussed in the first chapter of the book, which comprises half of the book's text. Teece stresses that

> " Dynamic capabilities can be disaggregated into the capacity to (1) sense and shape opportunities and threats, (2) to seize opportunities, and (3) to maintain competitiveness though enhancing, combining, protecting and when necessary, reconfiguring the business enterprise's intangible and tangible assets. "
>
> David Teece, *Dynamic Capabilities and Strategic Management: Organizing for Innovation and Growth*

organizations need to create, extend, and commercialize on their assets in line with emerging technological, social and political changes. The first part of the book outlines the book's structure, summarizing the conceptual model and nature of dynamic capabilities and their micro-foundations.

The second theme highlights the practical and theoretical contributions of entrepreneurs, leaders and managers not only inside the company, but also externally in economic systems. In this regard, Teece views managers and entrepreneurs as important in their ability to identify and capture new business opportunities, to orchestrate organizational assets and to create newer and more effective business models and organizational forms.

Third, he argues that unbiased decision-making needs to be achieved through the design of effective organizational structures and incentive programs. The fourth theme sets out his hope that the dynamic capabilities framework can help to develop a theory of strategy that regards strategic processes as evolutionary.

Exploring the Ideas

The main ideas in the work relate to Teece's theory of the development of dynamic capabilities and the micro-foundations that constitute this process. According to Teece, the first process in the dynamic capabilities framework—sensing—includes a number of microfoundations such as: processes to direct internal research and development and to select new technologies; tapping supplier and complementary innovation; harnessing developments in exogenous (growing by means of external factors and additions) science and technology, and identifying target market segments, allowing for changes in customers' needs.

The second process in the framework—seizing opportunities—involves elements such as the selection of product architectures and business models, the setting of enterprise boundaries, the management process of complements and business platforms, and the ability to avoid biases, delusion, deception and hubris. The third process in the framework is managing threats and reconfiguration of activities. Teece argues that this can be achieved by decentralization and decomposition of the firm's business structure, co-specialization, but also through knowledge management and good governance structure, which assist the flow of technology.

Each of these ideas complement the key themes set out in the work. This approach allows the reader to analyze its arguments in depth and to compare them with those of other works in the management and strategy field.

Language and Expression

Teece expresses a number of interesting ideas in *Dynamic Capabilities,* all of which are products of his own original thought. In the process of developing the dynamic capabilities framework, he explores in depth existing theories of strategic management in order to position his ideas on the limitation of some of these theories and the contributions of others.

The intellectual fit between the core themes in *Dynamic Capabilities* is well developed and presented in a lucid structure, even though most of the chapters in the book had originally been created as academic journal articles. The book starts with an outline of the first theme as described above, highlighting the importance of strategic management practices, structures and decisions in the development of the dynamic capabilities framework. The second chapter discusses the work's second theme, which discusses the practical and theoretical contributions of entrepreneurs, leaders and managers not only inside the company but also externally in economic systems. In the third chapter, Teece takes a closer look at the foundations of dynamic capabilities, including the implementation of effective incentive programs—the third theme of the book.

The remaining chapters discuss the essence of dynamic capabilities in the study of multinational companies (MNCs) and suggest future paths for study. Overall, the text and the author's ideas are easy to comprehend by both experts in the strategy field as well as practitioners. The language is concise and clear, which makes the book easy and pleasant to read. The footnotes throughout the book offer additional explanations and an opportunity to expand and clarify concepts and theory. Teece's work intends to help scholars to understand the foundations of long-term enterprise success while helping managers to delineate relevant strategic considerations and the priorities they must adapt to enhance enterprise performance.

NOTES

1   David J. Teece, *Dynamic Capabilities and Strategic Management: Organizing for Innovation and Growth* (New York: Oxford University Press, 2009), 3-64.

2   David J. Teece, *Dynamic Capabilities and Strategic Management: Organizing for Innovation and Growth* (New York: Oxford University Press, 2009), 159-160.

3   David J. Teece, *Dynamic Capabilities and Strategic Management: Organizing for Innovation and Growth* (New York: Oxford University Press, 2009), 65-81.

4   David J. Teece (with Mie Augier), *Dynamic Capabilities and Strategic Management: Organizing for Innovation and Growth* (New York: Oxford University Press, 2009), 82-112.

MODULE 6
SECONDARY IDEAS

KEY POINTS

- In a world of increasing competition, a highly skilled and knowledgeable workforce is essential for continuous innovation and market competitiveness.

- Teece places managers, organizational leaders and entrepreneurs at the center of the process of developing dynamic capabilities.

- His stress on the impact of cognitive and emotional capacities in the development processes of dynamic capabilities is of increasing relevance.

Other Ideas

In *Dynamic Capabilities and Strategic Management,* David Teece sets out a number of interesting subordinate ideas, which aim to extend and support his theorization of the dynamic capability framework. First, he places special attention on the role of managers in the dynamic capability process. He concludes that the entrepreneurial rather than the administrative functions of the management should be regarded as key to economic growth. In a world of increased competition, large as well as small companies would require a more highly skilled and knowledgeable work force, as this is the key to continuous innovation. Teece argues that the traditional employment relationship does not work for a highly skilled workforce. Company management would need to make sure that they are providing and nurturing a higher degree of autonomy, which is paramount for enhancing team productivity and a higher degree of accountability and personal motivation. In supporting these ideas, Teece studies and shares examples from international companies and professional management teams.

> ❝ Dynamic capabilities are an attempt to integrate modern management theory. The central element missing in the integration of theories is the under-theorized role of asset orchestrating managers. ❞
>
> Felix Arndt, *review of Dynamic Capabilities and Strategic Management: Organizing for Innovation and Growth.*

Another subordinate idea is that change can be hindered by cognitive limitations within the organization, or by framing biases that frequently result from existing routines in the company. Teece claims that effective managers' and top leaders' skills are essential in coping with these impediments, sustaining dynamic capabilities and achieving organizational change.

Teece shares also a number of subordinate ideas related to the role of business enterprise, its capabilities and its role in economic growth. He stresses that firms build capabilities by learning, by doing, and industrial research. Previous studies have focused mainly on emphasizing the importance of conducting economic analysis for understanding macro-economic factors. In contrast, Teece emphasizes the importance of focusing on micro factors such as continuous technological innovation for evaluating company and national competitiveness. He discusses the importance of firm networks in understanding sources of wealth and business enterprise competitiveness.

Exploring the Ideas

According to Teece, economic theory pays little attention to the practices of executive managers and their economic functions. In his view, with the exception of William Baumol,* an American economist best known for the theory of contestable markets, previous commentators have missed the way that in some cases managers can manage employees effectively, but in other situations their role may be "invisible."

In chapter 2 of the book, Teece discusses the role of the managers in the dynamic capability process. Teece argues that executive managers possess several essential roles that help avoid business-related failures. The roles he identifies are: (1) orchestrating of co-specialized assets; (2) selecting organizational and governance modes and incentive programs; (3) designing business models; (4) nurturing of change processes and routines; (5) making decisions about investment choices; (6) providing leadership, motivation, and vision; and (7) implementing and design of control and basic operations. According to Teece, the first six functions should be regarded as strategic and entrepreneurial, while viewing the last one should be characterized as purely operational.

With these ideas, where earlier views of management functions recognized only the operational activities of managers, Teece moves on to stress the importance of their strategic functions. Beyond the theoretical contribution that this represents, these ideas are extremely useful for business leaders, as they highlight the importance of building decentralized governance structures where middle managers have more freedom and power in making independent business decisions.

Overlooked

One aspect of Teece's framework that has not attracted a significant research attention early on, but that is seen as being more relevant today, is the importance of cognitive and emotional capacities in the development processes of dynamic capabilities. In their 2009 article entitled "Cognitive Dynamics of Capability Development Paths," Tomi Laamanen* and Johan Wallin*[1] provide empirical evidence for the contribution of managerial cognition in the capability development process, while Hodgkinson* and Healey*[2] highlight the importance of the emotional/affective and unconscious intuitive processes in the development of capabilities and strategic adaptation. Hodgkinson and Healey show how each of the processes necessary for the development of dynamic capabilities—sensing, seizing and reconfiguring—requires both emotional and cognitive capacities.

In his book, Teece spends considerable time discussing the role of top managers in sensing, seizing and reconfiguring, these being the organizational processes by which a company achieves sustainable competitive performance, in his view.

What is lacking is an analysis of the role of members of top management teams, as well as groups of managers, in these organizational processes. In a 2011 journal article, Krsto Pandza* and his colleagues explored this gap in Teece's analysis by focusing on the practices of groups of actors in a major pharmaceutical company.[3] Pandza claims that a group with a distinct perception of the strategic value of a capability is more likely to act autonomously with the aim of improving capability development. Moreover, in cases of higher dependency within the group and little authority in the organization, a group of actors tends to impact the development of organizational capabilities by developing creative and complex practices.

Further research into these neglected areas would clarify the microelements that contribute to the construction of dynamic capabilities. This would allow more precise mechanisms for detecting dynamic capabilities, especially in organizations that tend to experience turbulent change and variable corporate performance.

NOTES

1   Tomi Laamanen and Johan Wallin, "Cognitive Dynamics of Capability Development Paths," *Journal of Management Studies* 46, no. 6 (2009): 950–81.

2   Gerard P. Hodgkinson and Mark P. Healey, "Psychological Foundations of Dynamic Capabilities: Reflexion and Reflection in Strategic Management," *Strategic Management Journal* 32, no. 13 (2011): 1500–16.

3   Krsto Pandza, Terry A. Wilkins and Eva A. Alfoldi, "Collaborative Diversity in a Nanotechnology Innovation System: Evidence from the EU Framework Programme," *Technovation* 31, no. 9 (2011): 476–89.

MODULE 7
ACHIEVEMENT

KEY POINTS

- Teece's framework is of questionable value in the study of hyper-turbulent markets and environments, such as the global financial crisis of 2008.

- However, the work successfully integrates elements of several other management theories.

- The framework has been seen as a relevant analytical tool across disciplines such as technology management, entrepreneurship, and marketing studies.

Assessing the Argument

David J. Teece's *Dynamic Capabilities and Strategic Management* can be seen as relevant to the study of dynamic capabilities in relation to processes of similar technological change in different geographical contexts, at least with regard to Western countries.

However, the financial crisis* of 2008 has called into question some of the main theoretical foundations of the dynamic capabilities view. Some critics, like Richard J. Arend* and Philip Bromiley,*[1] have expressed doubts as to the applicability of the theory when studying extremely turbulent events such as financial crises. Studies on the development of dynamic capabilities and companies' sustainable performance can yield biased results, they claim, especially where companies tend to differ in their performances, because change processes tend to vary in intensity.

In contrast to the effect of temporal and social considerations, cultural variation seems to have little impact on the applicability and universality of Teece's dynamic capability view. His concept of

66 Teece provides a comprehensive overview of his recent and valuable research on dynamic capabilities. Most of the texts included made it through the review processes of high-quality scientific journals, thus meeting highest scientific standards. Although the book is mainly a summary of past efforts, it is a good starting point both for readers from research and practice to learn more about dynamic capabilities and strategic management. 99

Urs Fueglistaller and Thomas Schrettle, "Book Review of *Dynamic Capabilities & Strategic Management—Organizing for Innovation and Growth,*" *International Small Business Journal*

dynamic capabilities is closely interrelated with the notion of organizational change, but the literature in this field is highly fragmented, mainly due to the difficulty of measuring the relevant characteristics. Hypercompetitive market environments and financial turbulence require constant review of existing strategic frameworks and affect the different social environments in which companies operate. This may cause problems in the managerial orchestration of organizational assets across large enterprises, which in turn affect the development processes of dynamic capabilities.

Indeed, in hyper-turbulent markets, the universality of Teece's framework can be seen as questionable not merely within a particular industry or region, but within a single company. On a micro-level, companies can be regarded as constructs of various semi-socio-organizational boundaries, often differing in structure from one department to another. Change processes can happen at different times and on different scales within these boundaries, impacting the development of dynamic capabilities unevenly across the organization, and thus calling into question the universality of the framework even as applied to the study of a single setting.

To date, *Dynamic Capabilities* has not been criticized for its approach to specific cultural contexts. However, in the fields of strategy, management science and organizational studies, a growing number of studies on companies from emerging markets (Brazil, Russia, India, China, South Africa, for example) have shown inconsistencies with theories developed in a Western organizational context. Further research studies, applying the dynamic capabilities framework in emerging market settings, are needed in order to assess the applicability of Teece's work there.

Achievement in Context

Teece's research work, and in particular his concept of dynamic capabilities, has not only retained its relevance in the contemporary business research field but has also become the foundation for a growing number of studies exploring and advancing the dynamic capabilities view. The significance of *Dynamic Capabilities* can be seen in the numbers of times the work has been cited in the few years since its first publication. According to the Web of Knowledge and Google Scholar, it is not only Teece's most cited work, but also the most cited work on dynamic capabilities, with more than 13,500 citations.

The text's usefulness has been enhanced by the increasing interest in and critical debate of the work. While it has received criticism with regard to some elements of Teece's theoretical assumptions, the overall academic perception of the text remains positive. As well as the positive attributes of the concept in an academic sense, Teece's framework is highly regarded for its applicability to real-life managerial challenges.

While Teece's ability to integrate both practical and theoretical insights in an elaborated piece of work does not give *Dynamic Capabilities* unexpected relevance or applications, he does successfully meet the objective specified at the beginning of the text.

In contrast to other works in strategy and economics, which explore the concept of sustainable performance by focusing on only one aspect of a firm's management, Teece's idea of dynamic capabilities integrates elements of different modern management theories. This allows for the development of a consistent, coherent and practically effective framework for analyzing a company's competitiveness and performance. Furthermore, through his discussion of the micro-foundations of dynamic capabilities, Teece provides not only an interesting finding in its own right but also a future path for research in this domain. The book marks a significant advance in the fields of strategic management, corporate strategy, and economics, explaining the foundations and prerequisites of sustainable enterprise performance and competitiveness.

Limitations

Teece's work can be regarded as highly influential outside his main field of strategy and economics. A review of the management literature suggests that his conceptual framework of dynamic capabilities has been favored as a theoretical tool in fields such as technology management, entrepreneurship[2,3] and marketing studies.

Authors from other fields have adapted the dynamic capabilities framework in innovative ways that have allowed for insightful findings and contributions. For example, in the field of technology management, researchers have argued Teece's framework to be highly relevant for examining technology management,[4] and suggest how a combination of resources and processes is created, implemented and protected for different technology management activities.[5] In the field of marketing, researchers have applied Teece's theoretical assumptions to the study of channel transformation, and identify different dynamic capabilities in the channel-transformational strategies of companies in the business-to-business sector.[6]

However, David Teece fails to discuss issues related to a company's outdated competences and the problem of competency traps.[7] Business success depends on a company's core competency in a given industry. In order to maintain competencies, businesses invest both tangible and intangible resources. However, in cases where a company is focused solely on maintaining their core competency, ignoring industrial changes and changing customer preferences may hurt the business competitiveness. This can lead to competence trap. The Eastman Kodak Company* is an example of a company which has experienced a competence trap, being a late arrival to the digital photography industry.

One of Teece's objectives as set out in his work is for the dynamic capabilities framework to serve as a useful tool for both practitioners and academics from various fields. Therefore, studies in other fields can be taken as favorable for Teece, as they not only shed light on interesting issues in their own right but also enhance the understanding of the applicability of the framework to different research endeavors. Overall, the ideas of those researchers who have applied the dynamic capabilities framework in this way have been well received in their respective research fields.

NOTES

1   Richard J. Arend and Philip Bromiley, "Assessing the Dynamic Capabilities View: Spare Change, Everyone?" *Strategic Organization* 7, no. 1 (2009): 75.

2   Ari Jantunen et al., "Entrepreneurial Orientation, Dynamic Capabilities and International Performance," *Journal of International Entrepreneurship* 3, no. 3 (2005): 223–43.

3   Lance R. Newey and Shaker A. Zahra, "The Evolving Firm: How Dynamic and Operating Capabilities Interact to Enable Entrepreneurship," *British Journal of Management* 20(S1) (2009): S81–S100.

4   Dilek Cetindamar, Robert Phaal and David Probert, "Understanding Technology Management as a Dynamic Capability: A Framework for Technology Management Activities," *Technovation* 29, no. 4 (2009): 237–46.

5   Hanna-Kaisa Ellonen, Patrik Wikström and Ari Jantunen, "Linking Dynamic-Capability Portfolios and Innovation Outcomes," *Technovation* 29, no. 11 (2009): 753–62.

6   H. Wilson and Elizabeth Daniel, "The Multi-Channel Challenge: A Dynamic Capability Approach," *Industrial Marketing Management* 36, no. 1 (2007): 10–20.

7   Arndt, F. Book Review: David J. Teece Dynamic Capabilities and Strategic Management: Organizing for Innovation and Growth Oxford: Oxford University Press, 2009. 286pp., *Organization Studies*, (2011) 32, 4: 576-579.

MODULE 8
PLACE IN THE AUTHOR'S WORK

KEY POINTS

- The book's fundamental idea comes from a 1990 working paper in which Teece coined the term "dynamic capability" together with Gary Pisano and Amy Shuen.

- Teece's academic life has been oriented toward understanding the business firm and its role in the global economy.

- Today, his dynamic capability framework remains one of the most cited works and analytical tools in the strategy field.

Positioning

David Teece's *Dynamic Capabilities and Strategic Management* was written in Berkeley, California in 2009. However, the book's fundamental idea comes from a 1990 working paper in which Teece, together with Gary Pisano and Amy Shuen coined the term "dynamic capability." The scholars spent more than seven years working on the manuscript. After a number of rejections for publications, the paper was finally printed by invitation and published in *Strategic Management Journal*. It received the Strategic Management Society's best paper award in 2003.[1]

The book can be perceived as the product of a number of works authored or co-authored by Teece over the preceding 20 years, which have become some of the most cited works in business and economics worldwide. The first part of the book consists of five chapters which aim to shed light on the foundations, nature, boundary conditions, history and the role of management in the development process of

> ❝ Teece's new book, *Dynamic Capabilities and Strategic Management: Organizing for Innovation and Growth,* is an ambitious one. In this book, the author takes the first step in untangling superior enterprise performance. He provides insights for managers who want to act in more thoughtful and shrewd ways, and also for scholars, who may find the conceptual frame promising as they are invited to join a venture towards 'creating a knowledge based theory of the firm.' According to Teece, understanding competition and wealth creation is at the heart of a new theory of management called 'Dynamic Capabilities'. ❞
>
> Felix Arndt, *Dynamic Capabilities and Strategic Management: Organizing for Innovation and Growth, book review*

dynamic capabilities. Teece advances his earlier theorizations on the framework since it was first published, by referring to the work of other academics such as Constance E. Helfat* (2007) and Sidney G. Winter (2003). For example, Teece agrees with Helfat et al. (2007) who discuss two factors to be central for calibrating capabilities: (1) 'technical fitness' defined by how effectively a capability performs its function regardless of how well a capability enables the company to make a living and (2) 'evolutionary fitness,' referencing the selection environment and how well the capability enables a firm to make a living. According to Teece, both of these concepts are relevant when discussing dynamic capability view. He argues that dynamic capabilities assist in achieving the evolutionary fitness as discussed by Helfat and her colleagues.

The book also includes two chapters written with Mie Augier, with whom the author collaborates to advance earlier understanding about the historical roots of the concept.

Integration

Overall, Teece's intellectual life has had an overall thrust and coherence. His academic research has been oriented toward understanding the business firm and its role in the global economy. In a speech delivered upon acceptance of Doctor Honoris Causa from St Petersburg State University in 2002, Teece noted that his research in the previous 20 years had been focused on exploring the following research questions: (1) why do firms exist? (2) Why are they hierarchical? (3) Why do firms not outsource if markets are efficient? (4) Why are firms diversified if there are gains to specialization? (5) Why should economies of scale and scope lead to large diversified firms rather than strategic partnering? (6) If firms have know-how, where does that know-how reside? If it is merely in the minds of the employees, how can the firm prevent the employee from extracting all the value? (7) How can firms profit from innovation if they don't have strong intellectual property* (IP)?

In Teece's point of view, he has been able to make a contribution and provide answers to these simple yet fundamental questions by integrating theories and understandings from economic theory, organization theory, business history, resource-based view* and the economics of innovation with his own capability-based view.

Significance

Teece's *Dynamic Capabilities* can be regarded as a distillation of his life's work but also as a manifestation of later developments in his thinking. The book is significant as a starting point of reference for students and practitioners who would like to understand the dynamic capability concept and the theories behind its development.

Although Teece refers to different organizational science concepts and theorizations in order to position his work in the field, he starts the book with his latest thinking on the micro-foundations of dynamic capabilities, moving on to discuss their importance for the performance of contemporary multinational companies.

Teece's corpus is intellectually coherent and unified in both its presentation and the way it is discussed. *Dynamic Capabilities* draws on works he co-authored in 1994 with Gary Pisano, and in 1997 with Pisano and Amy Shuen. In these earlier collaborative works, Teece proposed three organizational processes—co-ordination, learning and reconfiguring—as being the core elements of dynamic capabilities. In *Dynamic Capabilities,* he regards them as subsets of the processes that support the development of dynamic capabilities—sensing threats, seizing opportunities and reconfiguring.

Teece's ideas have had a tremendous impact in the field of management and strategy. Dynamic capabilities theory is now widely used as a theoretical framework for exploring the change processes and practices of large international firms. Academic interest in dynamic capabilities theory has inspired a large number of works in this domain, resulting in a special issue of *Organization Science* on the subject, published in 2012.

Teece's intellectual journey is significant as his work has not only shed light on several under-researched themes in economics and strategy, but it has also served as a foundation for a number of young researchers in their exploration of organizational change and adaptation.

NOTES

1   Helfat, C. E. (2011), Dynamic Capabilities and Strategic Management: Organizing for Innovation and Growth. By David J. Teece. *R&D Management*, 41 (2): 217–218.

SECTION 3
IMPACT

MODULE 9
THE FIRST RESPONSES

KEY POINTS

- The theoretical and empirical foundations of dynamic capability theory have been frequently criticized.

- Teece responded to critics by revising his definition of the concept to include recent empirical and conceptual developments.

- A consensus on the conceptual development of Teece's framework has been reached in some but not all aspects of the critical dialogue.

Criticism

David Teece's work *Dynamic Capabilities and Strategic Management* has been subject to in-depth critical analysis which undoubtedly has enriched the study of dynamic capabilities and the author's latest theorizations on the topic. A review of the literature indicates one of the most frequent areas of criticism to be the theoretical and empirical foundation of the dynamic capability concept. According to a number of critics, based on Teece's definition it is hard to identify any company that possesses dynamic capabilities.[1,2]

The existence of dynamic capabilities in Teece's perspective is measured on the basis of continuous positive performance of the company in the marketplace. However, from the standpoint of his critics, one should be able to define dynamic capabilities not only during times of a company's growth but also in times of instability and change. In its current state, Teece's framework holds that dynamic capabilities can be observed only in companies with a long history of superior performance.

> ❝ If the dynamic capability view does not quickly develop a theoretical foundation, the field should move away from the dynamic capability view. ❞
>
> Richard Arend and Philip Bromiley, "Assessing the dynamic capability view: spare change, everyone?" *Strategic Organization Journal*

Another criticism of the dynamic theory framework is that it is unclear how it links to related or unrelated diversification, these being important factors for achieving superior company performance.[3] The integrative nature of the dynamic capabilities framework has also faced certain criticisms. In their 2009 review of the critiques, confusions, and unanswered questions of the dynamic capability view, Arend and Bromiley argue that many established concepts—for example absorptive capacity,* change management, organizational learning, strategic fit or first-mover advantage—share issues similar to those that the dynamic capabilities perspective addresses. In their view, the dynamic capability perspective should provide more innovative insights, rather than merely repeating the assumptions of existing theoretical foundations, if it is to be classified as a coherent and novel theoretical framework.

With the latest edition of *Dynamic Capabilities*, Teece responds to some of the issues highlighted by some critics. His attempt to shed more light on the microfoundations of the dynamic capabilities framework, and on its importance in studying multinational companies (MNCs), indicates both attentiveness to critical feedback and an intention to clarify existing theoretical confusions.

Responses

The concept of dynamic capabilities, as set out in Teece's earlier works, had been criticized as tautological. In response, he elaborates the definition of the concept in *Dynamic Capabilities* to take in the latest developments in the field. Where his earliest work defined dynamic capabilities as "the firm's ability to integrate, build and reconfigure internal and external competences to address rapidly changing environments,"[4] in his latest work he expands the concept, stating that "dynamic capabilities refer to the particular (non-imitability) capacity business enterprises possess to shape, reshape, configure, and reconfigure assets so as to respond to changing technologies and markets and escape the zero-profit condition."*[5] He further describes dynamic capability as the firm's ability to sense, seize and adapt in order to be able to generate and exploit its specific competences and to address its changing environment. He incorporates the definitions of David Collis* (1994)[6] and Sidney Winter (2003)[7] when elaborating the concept, to specify that dynamic capabilities tend to govern the rate of ordinary capabilities.

From all the critical views of Teece's work, the most persuasive critics' view is with regard to the definitional tautology of his core concept. Previous critics and new researchers in the field of corporate strategy and management science have received his elaborations in the definition of dynamic capabilities positively.

Teece has also revised and elaborated some of his views on the dynamic capabilities framework. In particular, he has tried to enhance the empirical and conceptual building blocks of the concept by clarifying some of his previous ideas and borrowing new insights from recent empirical studies. Overall, critics of the work have been influential to a certain degree. The development of the concept being still very recent, however, more work is required regarding its links with related or unrelated diversification of the company.

Conflict and Consensus

A consensus on the conceptual development of Teece's framework has been reached in some but not all aspects of the critical dialogue. One area in which tensions have eased is the development of a working definition of dynamic capability. Currently, there are a variety of conceptualizations and interpretations of how dynamic capabilities should be defined.

There has been a divergence in regards to finding the right definition of what dynamic capabilities are. A scan of the dynamic capability literature from 1994, when Teece published his first work on the topic, to date unveils three main propositions about the origins of dynamic capabilities. Dynamic capabilities have been argued to be composed of either organizational or managerial processes (e.g. Teece 1997), higher-level organizational routines (e.g. Collis, 1994, Winter 2003) or as a composition of both organizational processes and routines (Zollo and Winter, 2002).

Moreover, some critics hold that the integrative nature of Teece's dynamic capability framework, borrowing as it does from various concepts in the fields of management and strategy, produces confusion and cannot be characterized as an original theory. Teece, however, maintains that the integrative nature of the framework is precisely what enables it to enhance those fields.

NOTES

1   Oliver E. Williamson, "Strategy Research: Governance and Competence Perspectives," *Strategic Management Journal* 20, no. 12 (1999): 1087–1108.

2   Sidney G. Winter, "Understanding Dynamic Capabilities," *Strategic Management Journal* 24, no. 10 (2003): 991–5.

3   Richard J. Arend and Philip Bromiley, "Assessing the Dynamic Capabilities View: Spare Change, Everyone?" *Strategic Organization* 7, no. 1 (2009): 75.

4   David J. Teece, Gary Pisano and Amy Shuen, "Dynamic Capabilities and Strategic Management," *Strategic Management Journal* 18, no. 7 (1997): 516.

5   David J. Teece, *Dynamic Capabilities and Strategic Management: Organizing for Innovation and Growth* (New York: Oxford University Press, 2009), 47.

6   David J. Collis, "Research Note: How Valuable are Organizational Capabilities?" *Strategic Management Journal* 15(S1) (2006): 143–52.

7   Sidney G. Winter, "Understanding Dynamic Capabilities," *Strategic Management Journal* 24, no.10 (2003): 991–95.

MODULE 10
THE EVOLVING DEBATE

KEY POINTS

- *Dynamic Capabilities and Strategic Management* can be characterized as a "game-changer" in the management and strategy field.
- The dynamic capabilities view breaks with previously conventional models and theories.
- Two of Teece's most prominent followers are undoubtedly Gary Pisano and Amy Shuen.

Uses and Problems

David Teece's *Dynamic Capabilities and Strategic Management* has not only inspired and fueled a wide intellectual debate on the development processes and elements of the dynamic capability view, but has also inspired new avenues of research in the past decade. This is particularly true in the context of the development of organizational capabilities to allow a successful change in firm- specific organizational processes, and to achieve sustainable performance over time. A glance at the 2012 special issue of the *Journal of Management Studies*, dedicated to dynamic capabilities, indicates some of the key areas of his work which have attracted a large number of research studies, even as they continue to evolve and develop.

The idea of microfoundations for sensing, seizing and reconfiguring—the three processes that David Teece identifies as resulting in a company's dynamic capabilities—has been especially influential. In the past few years, researchers (such as Teppo Felin et al.)[1] have begun to explore in depth the micro components of dynamic capabilities—for example, individuals, social processes and

> ❝ Most of the debates have focused on two critical issues. The first concerns the nature of dynamic capabilities and the definition of the term; the second concerns their effects and consequences. These issues are interrelated and are key to developing, testing and applying the dynamic capabilities construct fruitfully. ❞
>
> Mark Easterby-Smith, Marjorie A. Lyles and Margaret A. Peteraf, *Dynamic Capabilities: Current Debates and Future Directions*

organizational structures—to explain competitive and organizational heterogeneity.

Moreover, some researchers have begun a close examination of these capabilities' micro-foundations, not by considering each of them in isolation but rather by examining the possible interactions and interrelationships between them. Another area that Teece touches upon indirectly in *Dynamic Capabilities,* but does not develop in depth, is the question of the institutional underpinnings of dynamic capabilities in multinational enterprises. His chapter on the essence of dynamic capabilities in particular inspired Dunning and Lundan[2] to examine how multinational enterprises can generate dynamic capabilities by combining locally embedded capabilities and mobile capabilities across borders.

Dynamic Capabilities can be characterized as a "game-changer" in the management and strategy field especially in the study of multinational enterprise performance. Teece's dynamic capabilities view breaks with previously conventional models and theories such as Michael Porter's Five Forces model, and highlights the shortcomings of other theoretical developments such as Penrose's resource-based view, to argue that the essence of strategy formulation is not "coping with competition," as Porter states, but rather the creation of business models and technologies that can sustain competitive advantages.

Schools of Thought

Since its first published description in 1997, Teece's dynamic capabilities view of the firm has influenced a wide community of researchers in strategy, economics and management science, who draw their inspiration from the view's theoretical assumptions and especially from Teece's more recent work on its conceptual underpinnings. One such researcher is Mie Augier, a scholar in the field of organizational theory and practice at Stanford University, whose interest in Teece's work resulted in her co-authorship of two chapters in the 2011 edition of *Dynamic Capabilities*. Other followers of Teece include such well-known scholars of strategy and international business as Sidney Winter, Maurizio Zollo,* Pisano and Shuen, David Collins, Constance Helfat and Margaret Peteraf,*[3] Nikolai Felin, and Teppo Foss.*

Two major schools of thought can be identified within the field of dynamic capabilities. The first, exemplified by Winter,[4] Zollo,[5] and Kathleen Eisenhardt* and Jeffrey Martin,*[6] tries to construct a clear definition which would simplify the operationalization of the concept for its research-based and practical implications. The second, notably represented by Giovanni Gavetti,*[7] Teppo Felin, and Nikolai Foss[8] is concerned with the further development of Teece's work on the microfoundations of dynamic capabilities.

Both groups of researchers have built on Teece's theoretical constructs to further develop the concept of dynamic capabilities, regarding the company's adaptation to technological or turbulent change. For example, representatives of the second school of thought have built on prior research to identify three main categories—individuals, social processes and organizational structures—which underlie the development of organizational and dynamic capabilities. Another kind of modernization of Teece's concept can be seen in its definitional conceptualizations: although Kathleen Eisenhardt and Jeffrey Martin's proposed definition of dynamic capabilities is similar to Teece's,[9] their reasoning on the conceptual link with the building of sustainable competitive advantage is slightly different. In their view, relating the dynamic capabilities of a firm to its competitive advantage is relevant only if the resource reconfigurations inside the capabilities themselves are further studied.

These ideas will in all probability serve as starting points for new thinking in the field of strategy and management, especially as it concerns dynamic capabilities and a company's sustainable competitive advantages.

In Current Scholarship

Since his first publication on the subject in a 1997 journal article and in particular in the book *Dynamic Capabilities* itself, Teece's work has influenced a number of scholars in the fields of organizational change and corporate strategy, who have followed key parts of his theoretical assumptions in their research. Two of his most prominent followers are undoubtedly Gary Pisano and Amy Shuen, with whom Teece co-wrote the 1997 article entitled "*Dynamic Capabilities and Strategic Management.*" Both authors share his ideas on the dynamic capabilities framework, especially his idea that in times of rapid technological change a company's wealth depends on its internal technological, managerial and organizational resources and processes, and its asset positions inside and outside the firm.

Teece has co-authored papers with several other researchers over the past few years—for example, Christos N. Pitelis* and Mie Augier—and his dynamic capability framework has been central to a wide range of intellectual works. Other disciples focus and attempt to build on a particular issue mentioned in Teece's work such as issues related to heterogeneous company performances within a single market of operations.[10]

In a similar vein, Pitelis collaborated with Teece in 2010 to extend the application of his work to the study of multinational companies (MNCs) and foreign direct investment. They argue that by focusing on important micro-foundations, as specified by Teece in his earlier work—for example, the role of entrepreneurial management in orchestrating system-wide value creation, through market and eco-system creation and co-creation—researchers can better understand the nature of MNCs in the global knowledge-based economy.

Furthermore, Teece's dynamic capability view has been also applied as an analytical framework in studies of companies from emerging markets such as China.[11] The modern trend towards close study of the micro-foundations of a firm's dynamic capabilities, as identified by Teece, has been highly influential in the field of strategy and international business. This has resulted in a number of special issues on the topic in the last few years, notably in *Organization Science* in 2012.

NOTES

1   Teppo Felin et al., "Microfoundations of Routines and Capabilities: Individuals, Processes, and Structure," *Journal of Management Studies* 49, no. 8 (2012): 1351–74.

2   John H. Dunning and Sarianna M. Lundan, *Multinational Enterprises and the Global Economy* (Cheltenham: Edward Elgar Publishing, 2008).

3   Constance E. Helfat and Margaret A. Peteraf, "The Dynamic Resource-Based View: Capability Lifecycles," *Strategic Management Journal* 24, no. 10 (2003): 997–1010.

4   Sidney G. Winter, "Dynamic Capabilities," *Strategic Management Journal* 24, no. 10 (2003): 991–95.

5   Maurizio Zollo and Sidney G. Winter, "Deliberate Learning and the Evolution of Dynamic Capabilities," *Organization Science* 13, no. 3 (2002): 339–51.

6   Kathleen M. Eisenhardt and Jeffrey A. Martin, "Dynamic Capabilities: What are They?" *Strategic Management Journal* 21, nos. 10-11 (2000): 1105–21.

7   Giovanni Gavetti, "Cognition and Hierarchy: Rethinking the Microfoundations of Capabilities' Development," *Organization Science* 16, no. 6 (2005): 599–617.

8   Teppo Felin et al., "Microfoundations of Routines and Capabilities: Individuals, Processes, and Structure," *Journal of Management Studies* 49, no. 8 (2012): 1351–74.

9   Kathleen M. Eisenhardt and Jeffrey A. Martin, "Dynamic Capabilities: What are They?" *Strategic Management Journal* 21, nos. 10-11 (2000): 1105–21.

10   David G. Hoopes and Tammy L. Madsen, "A Capability-Based View of Competitive Heterogeneity," *Industrial and Corporate Change* 17, no. 3 (2008): 393–426.

11   Lanlan Cao, "Dynamic Capabilities in a Turbulent Market Environment: Empirical Evidence from International Retailers in China." *Journal of Strategic Marketing* 19, no. 5 (2011): 455–69.

MODULE 11
IMPACT AND INFLUENCE TODAY

KEY POINTS

- *Dynamic Capabilities* is a seminal work that has had a strong impact in the strategic management field and enjoys a growing popularity across disciplines.

- Teece draws mostly with three approaches: the resource based view of the firm, the competitive forces approach, and game theory.

- Alternative perspectives are offered by organizational capability theory, contractual theory and industrial analysis.

Position

David Teece published his book *Dynamic Capabilities and Strategic Management* in 2010 after more than two decades of researching and publishing in the field of strategic management. It has a well-established position in the field. The book is a seminal work and presents a collection of high quality research articles on the notion of dynamic capability and a company sustainable performance.

The most heavily-researched question in the strategic management field concerns the firm process and practices of creating stakeholder wealth and sustaining competitiveness. In this intellectual debate, Teece's work on dynamic capability view has inspired significant scholarly attention and research effort. Today, dynamic capability view is one of the most used theoretical frameworks in the strategic management field for analyzing issues related to business competitiveness, business adoptability and change.

> **❝** Nearly two decades after first introducing the notion of dynamic capabilities in 1990, David J. Teece, doubtless one of the most prominent voices in strategic management research today, presents a view of his recent work... Teece offers a well-crafted overview of the last 20 years of his research. That is at least one reason why the book is a 'must' for scholars, researchers and practitioners who are interested in the micro-foundation of enterprise performance. **❞**
>
> Urs Fueglistaller and Thomas Schrettle, Book Review of *Dynamic Capabilities & Strategic Management—Organizing for Innovation and Growth, International Small Business Journal*

Teece's ideas have inspired a wide range of research work and continue to do so specifically since his call for more research attention on the role of entrepreneurial manager and entrepreneurial actions as central for the development of dynamic capability. To date, the dynamic capability view has inspired a number of highly cited journal articles and special issues. Interest in applying the dynamic capability view as an analytical tool has grown across disciplines, especially in entrepreneurship and technology management. International business scholars have also offered some insights into the role of dynamic capabilities in exploring and explaining the antecedents, processes, and consequences of international cross-collaborations. Recently, there has been a call for advancing knowledge and consolidating the fragmented literature in this field. The most recent special issue by the *Journal of International Business Studies* calls for making dynamic capabilities actionable for understanding nascent and established multinational enterprises in the international business field.

Interaction

When developing the dynamic capability framework, David Teece interacts mostly with three approaches; the resource based view of the firm, the competitive forces approach and game theoretic models. In his analysis of these approaches, Teece explains that each of them sees the strategic problem of securing sustainable performance and competitiveness in different yet complimentary ways. The competitive forces model tends to explain the strategic problem in terms of industry structure, entry deterrence, and positioning. The game-theoretic models define the strategic problem as one of interaction between rivals with certain expectations about how the other will behave. The resource-based perspective, on the other hand, defines success through the firm-specific assets which enable exploitation in the first place.

In contrast to these views, Teece argues that it is essential for identifying the micro-foundations upon which distinctive and non-imitable competences and capabilities can be developed, sustained, and improved.

Teece challenges in particular the static nature of the resource-based view of the firm. He argues that even if a company owns difficult to replicate assets, this is not sufficient for outperforming other market competitors in the long run. Companies which want to commercialize a continuous stream of innovation need to create, extend and protect their assets. According to Teece, companies operating in high technology industries such as IBM,* Texas Instruments,* and Philips* need to demonstrate timely responsiveness and rapid and flexible innovation, executed through effective coordination and internal and external competences if they want to secure longevity and competiveness in the long- term.

The Continuing Debate

Teece's *Dynamic Capabilities* is part of a long-standing debate in strategy and management science concerning the origins of a company's sustainable competitive advantage and performance. Although it is one of the latest theoretical developments in the attempt to understand competitiveness, a quick look at the management literature shows a lively and continuing intellectual debate over the theoretical underpinnings of a company's sustainable advantages.

The main debate appears to be between two schools of thought: on the one hand, proponents of organizational capability theory, and on the other, contractual theorists such as the transaction cost economist Oliver E. Williamson,[1] along with proponents of Michael Porter's[2] industrial analysis and of agency theory. Teece argues that contractual theorists tend to provide significant insight into the macro-level factors influencing a company's performance, but they do not go deep enough to identify the real components of a company's sustainable advantages.

Teece's work in this intellectual debate can be characterized as having a bridging effect, and his argument on the diversification and innovation boundaries of the firm help to link both organizational capability and contractual perspectives. Rather than opposing this argument, Williamson has agreed with Teece's position and modified his own earlier "efficiency hypothesis" accordingly.[3] In earlier versions of his work, Williamson argues that transactions tend to be linked with organizations that minimize transaction costs; later, he modifies this viewpoint to share Teece's perspective that the firm should be analyzed both as a contractual entity and as a set of capabilities. In contrast to Williamson, Porter has not responded formally to Teece's arguments, but he has focused his latest theoretical work on the link between sustainability practices and a company's competitive advantages.

Overall, the motivations of those who have responded to the challenges posed by Teece can be characterized as a mixture of intellectual, professional and to some extent personal. The professional aspect shows in their thoughtful approach to Teece's criticisms, and their capacity to enrich their previous arguments based on his feedback. Their intellectual motives are interrelated with their personal objectives of advancement in their theoretical field.

NOTES

1   Oliver E. Williamson, *The Economic Institutions of Capitalism* (New York: Free Press, 1985).

2   Michael E. Porter, "The Competitive Advantage of the Inner City," *Harvard Business Review* 73 (1995): 55–71.

3   Oliver E. Williamson, "Strategizing, Economizing, and Economic Organization," *Strategic Management Journal* 2d ser., 12 (1991): 75–94.

MODULE 12
WHERE NEXT?

KEY POINTS

* Teece's core ideas are likely to be further developed – in particular the idea of the micro-foundations of dynamic capabilities.

* The close study of the micro-foundations, urged by Teece, has become highly influential in the fields of strategy and international business.

* Teece's work helps to explain how companies can change and adapt during turbulent times to sustain their competitive advantages.

Potential

With a current environment characterized by turbulent change due to financial crises, increasing technological innovation and hyper competition caused by rapid internationalization from emerging market countries, David J. Teece's *Dynamic Capabilities and Strategic Management* is likely to be highly influential in future. Two factors tend to favor this outcome: Teece's status as the pioneer of the concept of dynamic capabilities, and the text's innovative attempt to explain a company's sustainable performance and competitive advantage by linking the theory of the firm with the study of economic development.

An overview of the current debate in the dynamic capabilities literature, taken together with an evaluation of the socio-economic environment, highlights certain of Teece's core ideas as likely to be further developed by researchers in the field, in particular the idea of the micro-foundations of dynamic capabilities. Recent research has

> **" Teece** points out ... such a (interdisciplinary, yet disciplined) vision is the first step toward realizing a coherent program in strategic management; and we may see the dynamic capability program as taking the first important steps toward establishing a coherent and rigorous research program in strategic management. **"**
>
> Mie Augier, *The Evolving Dynamics of Organizational Capabilities: An interview with David J. Teece*

focused on the development of organizational and dynamic capabilities by separate study on different levels of determinants such as processes, structure and individuals. For example, other research studies have explored the individual-level determinants of strategic dynamic capabilities in subsidiaries of multinational companies (MNCs).[1] More research can be expected regarding the cognitive dimensions of individual level components such as managerial foresight and cognition.

Despite several years of subsequent research on organizational routines and capabilities, *Dynamic Capabilities* has not lost its relevance. This can be attributed to the book's integrative nature, drawing on economics, organizational behavior, corporate strategy and decision-making theory, as well as the highly turbulent business ecosystem in which company executives and entrepreneurs make their day-to-day decisions. The financial crisis that started in 2008, and the challenges it has posed to many businesses around the world, support Teece's viewpoint. Nowadays, it is not sufficient, he argues, to take an industry as a unit of analysis: researchers should focus on exploring the relationship between different stakeholders of the business ecosystem, and the specifics of the company itself, in order to understand in depth the sources of its competitiveness.

Overall, Teece's ideas are still relevant, and are likely to be of continuing importance in the coming years of increasing global competition and organizational changes.

Future Directions

Since his first publication on the subject in a 1997 journal article and in particular in *Dynamic Capabilities*, Teece's work on dynamic capabilities has influenced a number of scholars in the fields of organizational change and corporate strategy, who have followed key parts of his theoretical assumptions in their research. Gary Pisano and Amy Shuen share his ideas on the dynamic capabilities framework, especially his idea that in times of rapid technological change a company's wealth depends on its internal technological, managerial and organizational resources and processes, and its asset positions inside and outside the firm.

David Teece has collaborated with a wide range of scholars representing different disciplines such as Christos N. Pitelis and Mie Augier, to produce a wide range intellectual works. Other disciples focus and attempt to build on a particular issue mentioned in Teece's work, such as issues related to heterogeneous company performances within a single market of operations.

In a similar vein, Pitelis collaborated with Teece in 2010 to extend the application of his work to the study of multinational companies (MNCs) and foreign direct investment. They argue that by focusing on important micro-foundations, as specified by Teece in his earlier work, for example, the role of entrepreneurial management in orchestrating system-wide value creation, through market and eco-system creation and co-creation, researchers can better understand the nature of MNCs in the global knowledge-based economy.

Furthermore, authors have applied Teece's dynamic capability view as an analytical framework in the study of companies from emerging markets. In particular, by using Teece's vocabulary, researchers have explored how an international retailer from China can build and classify its dynamic capabilities in a turbulent foreign market. The modern trend towards close study of the micro-foundations of a firm's dynamic capabilities, as identified by Teece, has been highly influential in the field of strategy and international business. Teppo Felin and Nikolai Foss have tried to extend our understanding of organizational capabilities further by underlying their micro-level components such as individuals, social, processes, and structure.

Summary

Teece's book *Dynamic Capabilities and Strategic Management* deserves the attention of the research community, and it can be classified as a seminal work in the fields of strategy, economics and management science. It builds upon a number of disciplines such as strategy, decision-making, organizational science, management and economics, as well as theories such as transaction-cost economics, the resource-based theory of the firm and evolutionary economics. By combining management theories with social science disciplines, it provides insights for students, academics and practitioners who are looking for an understanding of competition and wealth creation. Teece's work also stands out for its analysis of the challenges that multinational companies (MNCs) tend to face in the contemporary knowledge-based economy, especially in terms of sustaining their competitive advantages.

The text is original both in its structure and its theoretical development. Its considerable impact in the field of strategy and management science can be attributed to the central contribution of Teece's work, his development of the dynamic capabilities framework, which helps to explain how companies can change and adapt during turbulent times to sustain their competitive advantages. The three processes identified by Teece—sensing, seizing and reconfiguring—have become a frequently used analytical framework for researchers interested in the study of organizational change. His work is likely to be of continuing importance for its theoretical contribution to the fields of strategy, economics, management science, and international business, and it seems certain to maintain its influence on the research of dynamic capabilities and organizational change, particularly the development of dynamic capabilities over time.

The book features in-depth discussion on the origins of competitive advantage, and the importance of internal issues for building and maintaining dynamic capabilities, which Teece regards as vital for companies to thrive and survive through turbulent times. This emphasis sets the text apart from previously introduced theories, such as Penrose's resource-based theory of the firm, Porter's Five Forces model or transaction-cost theory, which have focused mainly on the external issues faced by firms. The uniqueness of Teece's work lies in the way his research embraces different aspects and levels of the organization. It also helps managers consider different strategic issues and set the necessary priorities to escape the zero-profit tendency and adapt to technological and organizational changes.

NOTES

1   Kristiina Mäkelä et al., "Determinants of Strategic HR Capabilities in MNC Subsidiaries," *Journal of Management Studies* 49, no. 8 (2012): 1459–83.

GLOSSARY

GLOSSARY OF TERMS

Absorptive capacity describes a firm's potential to apply useful external knowledge, first through successful identification, then assimilation, and finally transformation for its own ends.

Contestable market theory is an economic concept associated with the American economist William Baumol. It refers to a market with zero entry and zero exit costs such as sunk costs and contractual agreements.

Dynamic capability: The term dynamic capability refers to the particular capacity business enterprises possess to shape, reshape, configure, and reconfigure assets in order to respond to changes in the marketplace and escape the zero-profit condition.

Eastman Kodak Company is an American technology company that primarily manufactures products related to the field of photography. In recent years, it has become known for its adherence to products that were becoming rapidly obsolete and a failure to develop successful new lines of products, particularly with the onset of digital camera technology.

Economies of scale: Economies of scale refer to the reduction of the average cost of production as the number of units of a given product type is increased.

Economies of scope: Economies of scope refer to the reduction of the average cost of production as the number of product types is increased.

Evolutionary Economics is a part of the mainstream economics field. It focuses on the study of processes that transforms the economy of firms, institutions, employment, trade, and production based on individual actors' actions, interactions and experience.

Exogenous: Growing by means of external factors and additions.

Financial Crisis is a situation in which the value of financial institutions or assets drop rapidly and lose a large part of their normal value.

Five-Forces Model: A framework developed by Professor Michael Porter in 1979 to understand the competitive forces which exist in a given industry and help determine its weaknesses and strengths. These five forces are: bargaining power of suppliers, bargaining power of customers, threat of substitute products, industry rivalry, and threat of new entrants into the industry.

Game theory is a mathematical field of study in which the outcomes of competitive situations involving the actions of single or multiple participants are analyzed for likelihood of occurrence.

Hypercompetitive environment (hypercompetition) is an environment where there is a lot of very strong competition between companies. In such environments, markets tend to change very fast, new competitors can enter the market quickly, making it difficult for one company to sustain their competitive advantage for a long time.

IBM (International Business Machines Corporations) Founded in 1911, IBM is one of the world's oldest computing companies, and it is today one of the world's largest employers. It has remained successful for over a century by constantly shifting its business focus and divesting older product lines as new markets emerge.

Intellectual property (IP) refers to a category of property which includes intangible creations such as copyrights, patents, trademarks.

Microfoundations in the field of economics refer to the microeconomic analysis of the behavior of individual agents such as households or firms that underpins a macroeconomic theory.

Microfoundations of dynamic capabilities refer to the distinct skills, processes, procedures, organizational structures, decision rules, and disciplines which support the company in sensing, seizing, and reconfiguring capacities.

Multinational company (MNC) is a company which has facilities and assets in at least one country other than its home country.

Neo-Schumpeterian theory: The neo-Schumpeterian theory of the firm refers to Sidney Winter's proposal for a further development of Joseph Schumpeter's theory.

Philips is a multinational technology company, founded and headquartered in Amsterdam, which has product divisions in electronics, lighting, and healthcare.

Resource-based view: The resource-based view of the firm refers to the view that a company's competitive advantage depends on whether the firm has valuable, inimitable, rare, or non-substitutable resources.

Scale-based facilities: Scale-based facilities are defined here as the facilities that enable a given enterprise to establish contracts (external buyers, for example) that would increase the scale of its business.

Texas Instruments is an American technology company that primarily produces specialized supply parts for a global clientele of electronics designers and manufacturers. Texas Instruments developed the first successful hand held calculator in the 1960s, but since then has continued to develop and modernize its product line for the 21st century, and it is currently among the top ten suppliers of semiconductors in the world.

Transaction-cost economics is theory in the field of Strategy. It is interested in explaining why firms exist in the first place (i.e., to minimize transaction costs), how firms define their boundaries, and how they ought to govern operations.

Zero-profit condition refers to the condition in which an industry or a business has extremely low or near zero cost of entry.

PEOPLE MENTIONED IN THE TEXT

Veronique Ambrosini is the Head of Department, Professor of Management (Strategic Management) at Monash Business School.

Richard J. Arend is Professor of Strategy and Entrepreneurship at the Henry W. Bloch School of Management, University of Missouri—Kansas City in the United States.

Mie Augier is a senior consulting researcher at Stanford University at the center for sustainable development and global competitiveness. She is author of more than 70 articles and books in the field of strategic management and organizational decision-making.

Jay Barney (b.1954) is an American professor in strategic management best known for his contributions to the resource-based theory of competitive advantage.

William Baumol is an American economist who is best known for the theory of contestable markets, the Baumol–Tobin model of money demand.

Philip Bromiley is Dean's Professor in Strategic Management at UCI Paul Merage School of Business in the United States.

David Collis is currently the Thomas Henry Carroll Ford Foundation Adjunct Professor of Business Administration within the strategy unit at Harvard Business School. He was previously a professor at the Yale School of Management and at Columbia Business School.

Kathleen Eisenhardt is the Stanford W. Ascherman M.D. Professor and Co-Director of the Stanford Technology Ventures Program. Her research focus is strategy and organization, especially in technology-based companies and high-velocity industries.

Teppo Felin is a Professor of Strategy at Saïd Business School, University of Oxford. His areas of expertise include strategy, entrepreneurship and innovation, complex systems, and competitive advantage.

Nicolai J. Foss is a Danish organizational theorist and entrepreneurship scholar, and The Rodolfo de Benedetti Chaired Professor of Entrepreneurship at the Bocconi University.

Giovanni Gavetti is an Associate Professor of Business Administration at the Tuck School of Business at University of Dartmouth.

Mark P. Healey is an Associate Professor in Strategic Management at Manchester Business School. He received his Ph.D. in Management Sciences from the University of Manchester Institute of Science and Technology (UMIST).

Constance E. Helfat is J. Brian Quinn Professor in Technology and Strategy at the University of Dartmouth, Tuck Business School. Her research seeks to understand the nature of strategic change in organizations, particularly change that is a result of emerging technology, knowledge, and capabilities.

Gegard P. Hodgkinson is Vice Dean for Research of the Faculty of Humanities and Professor of Strategic Management and Behavioral Science at the University of Manchester Business School in the United Kingdom.

Tomi Laamanen is Chaired Professor of Strategic Management, Director of the Institute of Management, Director of the PhD Program of Management, and Academic Director of the Strategy and International Management Master (SIM) Program of the University of St.Gallen.

Edwin Mansfield (1930–1997) was a leading economic analyst and professor, exploring the economics of technological change. He published more than 200 articles and 30 books in the field of economics.

Jeffrey Martin is an Associate Professor of Management at the University of Alabama Culverhouse School of Business. He received his Ph.D. in Strategy and Organization from Stanford University in 2002. He has published his work in leading management journals including the *Strategic Management Journal*, *Academy of Management Journal*, Organization Science, and Strategic Organization. His research is internationally recognized in the area of dynamic capabilities and his paper "Dynamic Capabilities: What Are They?" won the Dan and Mary Lou Schendel Best Paper Award for *Strategic Management Journal* in 2007.

Krsto Pandza is Professor in Strategy and Innovation and the head of Strategy and Organization Group at the University of Leeds, Business School in the United Kingdom.

Edith Penrose was the creator of the resource-based theory of the firm. She referred to the firm as a "pool of resources, the utilization of which is organized in an administrative framework."

Margaret Peteraf is the Leon E. Williams Professor of Management at the Tuck School of Business at University of Dartmouth.

Gary Pisano is a professor of Business Administration at Harvard Business School. His research is in the field of technology strategy, the management of innovation, organizational learning, outsourcing, and the management of intellectual property.

Christos N. Pitelis is a Professor in of Strategy and Sustainable Competitiveness and University Ambassador (Business Research and Engagement) at Brunel University London, United Kingdom.

Michael Porter (b. May 23, 1947) is an American academic, currently professor at Harvard Business School, and known as the founder of modern strategy field and theories such as Porter's Hypothesis, Porter's Five Forces model, Porter's Four Corners analysis. He is one of the world's most influential thinkers on business competitiveness and management.

Amy Shuen is a global business and technology strategist and currently an author at Web 2.0 and Silicon Valley Digital Strategy Consulting.

Harbir Singh is a professor of management in Wharton School of Management. His research areas of interest focus on management of technological innovation, routines, learning and capability development.

Johan Wallin is an academic at the University of Gothenburg, Sweden.

Oliver E. Williamson is an American economist, most known for his work on transaction cost economics. He is a professor at the University of California, Berkeley and the recipient of the Nobel Memorial Prize in Economics Sciences in 2009.

Sidney G. Winter is a Deloitte and Touche Professor Emeritus of Management at the Wharton School of Business. His research areas are in the field of evolutionary economics and change.

Maurizio Zollo is Dean's Chaired Professor in Strategy and Sustainability at the Management and Technology department of Bocconi University and a board member of the Center for Research in Innovation, Organization and Strategy (CRIOS).

WORKS CITED

WORKS CITED

Ambrosini, Veronique, and Cliff Bowman. "What Are Dynamic Capabilities and are They a Useful Construct in Strategic Management?" *International Journal of Management Reviews* 11, no. 1 (2009): 29–49.

Arend, Richard J., and Philip Bromiley. "Assessing the Dynamic Capabilities View: Spare Change, Everyone?" *Strategic Organization* 7, no. 1 (2009): 75.

Augier, Mie-Sophia. *The Evolving Dynamics of Organizational Capabilities: An Interview with David J. Teece.* København. (2004): 36.

Cao, Lanlan. "Dynamic Capabilities in a Turbulent Market Environment: Empirical Evidence from International Retailers in China." *Journal of Strategic Marketing* 19, no. 5 (2011): 455–69.

Cetindamar, Dilek, Robert Phaal and David Probert. "Understanding Technology Management as a Dynamic Capability: A Framework for Technology Management Activities." *Technovation* 29, no. 4 (2009): 237–46.

Collis, David J. "Research Note: How Valuable are Organizational Capabilities?" *Strategic Management Journal*, 15 (2006): 143–52.

Dunning, John H., and Sarianna M. Lundan. *Multinational Enterprises and the Global Economy.* Cheltenham: Edward Elgar Publishing, 2008.

Eisenhardt, Kathleen M., and Jeffrey A. Martin. "Dynamic Capabilities: What are They?" *Strategic Management Journal* 21, nos. 10–11 (2000): 1105–21.

Ellonen, Hanna-Kaisa, Patrik Wikström and Ari Jantunen. "Linking Dynamic-Capability Portfolios and Innovation Outcomes." *Technovation* 29, no. 11 (2009): 753–62.

Felin, Teppo, Nicolai J. Foss, Koen H. Heimeriks and Tammy L. Madsen. "Microfoundations of Routines and Capabilities: Individuals, Processes, and Structure." *Journal of Management Studies* 49, no. 8 (2012): 1351–74.

Gavetti, Giovanni. "Cognition and Hierarchy: Rethinking the Microfoundations of Capabilities' Development." *Organization Science* 16, no. 6 (2005): 599–617.

Helfat, Constance E., and Margaret A. Peteraf. "The Dynamic Resource-Based View: Capability Lifecycles." *Strategic Management Journal* 24, no. 10 (2003): 997–1010.

Hodgkinson, Gerard P., and Mark P. Healey. "Psychological Foundations of Dynamic Capabilities: Reflexion and Reflection in Strategic Management." *Strategic Management Journal* 32, no. 13 (2011): 1500–16.

Hoopes, David G., and Tammy L. Madsen. "A Capability-Based View of Competitive Heterogeneity." *Industrial and Corporate Change* 17, no. 3 (2008): 393–426.

Hymer, Stephen. "The Efficiency (Contradictions) of Multinational Corporations." *American Economic Review* 60, no. 2 (1970): 441–8.

Hayek, Friedrich A. "The Use of Knowledge in Society." *The American Economic Review* 35, no. 4 (1945): 519–30.

Jantunen, Ari, Kaisu Puumalainen, Sami Saarenketo and Kalevi Kyläheiko. "Entrepreneurial Orientation, Dynamic Capabilities and International Performance." *Journal of International Entrepreneurship* 3, no. 3 (2005): 223–43.

Katkalo, Valery S., Christos N. Pitelis and David J. Teece. "Introduction: On the Nature and Scope of Dynamic Capabilities." *Industrial and Corporate Change* 19, no. 4 (2010): 1175–86.

Laamanen, Tomi, and Johan Wallin. "Cognitive Dynamics of Capability Development Paths." *Journal of Management Studies* 46, no. 6 (2009): 950–81.

Mäkelä, Kristiina, Jennie Sumelius, Mathias Höglund and Catarina Ahlvik. "Determinants of Strategic HR Capabilities in MNC Subsidiaries." *Journal of Management Studies* 49, no. 8 (2012): 1459–83.

Newey, Lance R., and Shaker A. Zahra. "The Evolving Firm: How Dynamic and Operating Capabilities Interact to Enable Entrepreneurship." *British Journal of Management* 20 (2009): S81–S100.

Pandza, Krsto, Terry A. Wilkins and Eva A. Alfoldi. "Collaborative Diversity in a Nanotechnology Innovation System: Evidence from the EU Framework Programme." *Technovation* 31, no. 9 (2011): 476–89.

Penrose, Edith. *The Theory of the Growth of the Firm.* Oxford: Oxford University Press, 2009 [1959].

Porter, Michael E. "The Competitive Advantage of the Inner City." *Harvard Business Review* 73 (1995): 55–71.

Teece, David J. *Dynamic Capabilities and Strategic Management: Organizing for Innovation and Growth.* New York: Oxford University Press, 2011 [2009].

Teece, David J. and Gary Pisano. "The Dynamic Capabilities of Firms: An Introduction." *Industrial and Corporate Change,* 3, no. 3 (1994): 537–56.

Teece, David J., Gary Pisano and Amy Shuen. "Dynamic Capabilities and Strategic Management." *Strategic Management Journal* 18, no. 7 (1997): 509–33.

Simon, Herbert A. "Near Decomposability and the Speed of Evolution." *Industrial and Corporate Change* 11, no. 3 (2002): 587–99.

Williamson, Oliver E. *The Economic Institutions of Capitalism*. New York: Free Press, 1985.

"Strategizing, Economizing, and Economic Organization." *Strategic Management Journal*, 2d ser., 12 (1991): 75–94.

"Strategy Research: Governance and Competence Perspectives." *Strategic Management Journal* 20, no. 12 (1999): 1087–1108.

Wilson, H., and Elizabeth Daniel. "The Multi-Channel Challenge: A Dynamic Capability Approach." *Industrial Marketing Management* 36, no. 1 (2007): 10–20.

Winter, Sidney G. "Understanding Dynamic Capabilities." *Strategic Management Journal* 24, no. 10 (2003): 991–5.

Zahra, Shaker A., Harry J. Sapienza and Per Davidsson. "Entrepreneurship and Dynamic Capabilities: A Review, Model and Research Agenda." *Journal of Management Studies* 43, no. 4 (2006): 917–55.

Zollo, Maurizio, and Sidney G. Winter. "Deliberate Learning and the Evolution of Dynamic Capabilities." *Organization Science* 13, no. 3(2002): 339–51.

THE MACAT LIBRARY
BY DISCIPLINE

AFRICANA STUDIES

Chinua Achebe's *An Image of Africa: Racism in Conrad's Heart of Darkness*
W. E. B. Du Bois's *The Souls of Black Folk*
Zora Neale Huston's *Characteristics of Negro Expression*
Martin Luther King Jr's *Why We Can't Wait*
Toni Morrison's *Playing in the Dark: Whiteness in the American Literary Imagination*

ANTHROPOLOGY

Arjun Appadurai's *Modernity at Large: Cultural Dimensions of Globalisation*
Philippe Ariès's *Centuries of Childhood*
Franz Boas's *Race, Language and Culture*
Kim Chan & Renée Mauborgne's *Blue Ocean Strategy*
Jared Diamond's *Guns, Germs & Steel: the Fate of Human Societies*
Jared Diamond's *Collapse: How Societies Choose to Fail or Survive*
E. E. Evans-Pritchard's *Witchcraft, Oracles and Magic Among the Azande*
James Ferguson's *The Anti-Politics Machine*
Clifford Geertz's *The Interpretation of Cultures*
David Graeber's *Debt: the First 5000 Years*
Karen Ho's *Liquidated: An Ethnography of Wall Street*
Geert Hofstede's *Culture's Consequences: Comparing Values, Behaviors, Institutes and Organizations across Nations*
Claude Lévi-Strauss's *Structural Anthropology*
Jay Macleod's *Ain't No Makin' It: Aspirations and Attainment in a Low-Income Neighborhood*
Saba Mahmood's *The Politics of Piety: The Islamic Revival and the Feminist Subjec*t
Marcel Mauss's *The Gift*

BUSINESS

Jean Lave & Etienne Wenger's *Situated Learning*
Theodore Levitt's *Marketing Myopia*
Burton G. Malkiel's *A Random Walk Down Wall Street*
Douglas McGregor's *The Human Side of Enterprise*
Michael Porter's *Competitive Strategy: Creating and Sustaining Superior Performance*
John Kotter's *Leading Change*
C. K. Prahalad & Gary Hamel's *The Core Competence of the Corporation*

CRIMINOLOGY

Michelle Alexander's *The New Jim Crow: Mass Incarceration in the Age of Colorblindness*
Michael R. Gottfredson & Travis Hirschi's *A General Theory of Crime*
Richard Herrnstein & Charles A. Murray's *The Bell Curve: Intelligence and Class Structure in American Life*
Elizabeth Loftus's *Eyewitness Testimony*
Jay Macleod's *Ain't No Makin' It: Aspirations and Attainment in a Low-Income Neighborhood*
Philip Zimbardo's *The Lucifer Effect*

ECONOMICS

Janet Abu-Lughod's *Before European Hegemony*
Ha-Joon Chang's *Kicking Away the Ladder*
David Brion Davis's *The Problem of Slavery in the Age of Revolution*
Milton Friedman's *The Role of Monetary Policy*
Milton Friedman's *Capitalism and Freedom*
David Graeber's *Debt: the First 5000 Years*
Friedrich Hayek's *The Road to Serfdom*
Karen Ho's *Liquidated: An Ethnography of Wall Street*

John Maynard Keynes's *The General Theory of Employment, Interest and Money*
Charles P. Kindleberger's *Manias, Panics and Crashes*
Robert Lucas's *Why Doesn't Capital Flow from Rich to Poor Countries?*
Burton G. Malkiel's *A Random Walk Down Wall Street*
Thomas Robert Malthus's *An Essay on the Principle of Population*
Karl Marx's *Capital*
Thomas Piketty's *Capital in the Twenty-First Century*
Amartya Sen's *Development as Freedom*
Adam Smith's *The Wealth of Nations*
Nassim Nicholas Taleb's *The Black Swan: The Impact of the Highly Improbable*
Amos Tversky's & Daniel Kahneman's *Judgment under Uncertainty: Heuristics and Biases*
Mahbub Ul Haq's *Reflections on Human Development*
Max Weber's *The Protestant Ethic and the Spirit of Capitalism*

FEMINISM AND GENDER STUDIES

Judith Butler's *Gender Trouble*
Simone De Beauvoir's *The Second Sex*
Michel Foucault's *History of Sexuality*
Betty Friedan's *The Feminine Mystique*
Saba Mahmood's *The Politics of Piety: The Islamic Revival and the Feminist Subject*
Joan Wallach Scott's *Gender and the Politics of History*
Mary Wollstonecraft's *A Vindication of the Rights of Woman*
Virginia Woolf's *A Room of One's Own*

GEOGRAPHY

The Brundtland Report's *Our Common Future*
Rachel Carson's *Silent Spring*
Charles Darwin's *On the Origin of Species*
James Ferguson's *The Anti-Politics Machine*
Jane Jacobs's *The Death and Life of Great American Cities*
James Lovelock's *Gaia: A New Look at Life on Earth*
Amartya Sen's *Development as Freedom*
Mathis Wackernagel & William Rees's *Our Ecological Footprint*

HISTORY

Janet Abu-Lughod's *Before European Hegemony*
Benedict Anderson's *Imagined Communities*
Bernard Bailyn's *The Ideological Origins of the American Revolution*
Hanna Batatu's *The Old Social Classes And The Revolutionary Movements Of Iraq*
Christopher Browning's *Ordinary Men: Reserve Police Batallion 101 and the Final Solution in Poland*
Edmund Burke's *Reflections on the Revolution in France*
William Cronon's *Nature's Metropolis: Chicago And The Great West*
Alfred W. Crosby's *The Columbian Exchange*
Hamid Dabashi's *Iran: A People Interrupted*
David Brion Davis's *The Problem of Slavery in the Age of Revolution*
Nathalie Zemon Davis's *The Return of Martin Guerre*
Jared Diamond's *Guns, Germs & Steel: the Fate of Human Societies*
Frank Dikotter's *Mao's Great Famine*
John W Dower's *War Without Mercy: Race And Power In The Pacific War*
W. E. B. Du Bois's *The Souls of Black Folk*
Richard J. Evans's *In Defence of History*
Lucien Febvre's *The Problem of Unbelief in the 16th Century*
Sheila Fitzpatrick's *Everyday Stalinism*

Eric Foner's *Reconstruction: America's Unfinished Revolution, 1863-1877*
Michel Foucault's *Discipline and Punish*
Michel Foucault's *History of Sexuality*
Francis Fukuyama's *The End of History and the Last Man*
John Lewis Gaddis's *We Now Know: Rethinking Cold War History*
Ernest Gellner's *Nations and Nationalism*
Eugene Genovese's *Roll, Jordan, Roll: The World the Slaves Made*
Carlo Ginzburg's *The Night Battles*
Daniel Goldhagen's *Hitler's Willing Executioners*
Jack Goldstone's *Revolution and Rebellion in the Early Modern World*
Antonio Gramsci's *The Prison Notebooks*
Alexander Hamilton, John Jay & James Madison's *The Federalist Papers*
Christopher Hill's *The World Turned Upside Down*
Carole Hillenbrand's *The Crusades: Islamic Perspectives*
Thomas Hobbes's *Leviathan*
Eric Hobsbawm's *The Age Of Revolution*
John A. Hobson's *Imperialism: A Study*
Albert Hourani's *History of the Arab Peoples*
Samuel P. Huntington's *The Clash of Civilizations and the Remaking of World Order*
C. L. R. James's *The Black Jacobins*
Tony Judt's *Postwar: A History of Europe Since 1945*
Ernst Kantorowicz's *The King's Two Bodies: A Study in Medieval Political Theology*
Paul Kennedy's *The Rise and Fall of the Great Powers*
Ian Kershaw's *The "Hitler Myth": Image and Reality in the Third Reich*
John Maynard Keynes's *The General Theory of Employment, Interest and Money*
Charles P. Kindleberger's *Manias, Panics and Crashes*
Martin Luther King Jr's *Why We Can't Wait*
Henry Kissinger's *World Order: Reflections on the Character of Nations and the Course of History*
Thomas Kuhn's *The Structure of Scientific Revolutions*
Georges Lefebvre's *The Coming of the French Revolution*
John Locke's *Two Treatises of Government*
Niccolò Machiavelli's *The Prince*
Thomas Robert Malthus's *An Essay on the Principle of Population*
Mahmood Mamdani's *Citizen and Subject: Contemporary Africa And The Legacy Of Late Colonialism*
Karl Marx's *Capital*
Stanley Milgram's *Obedience to Authority*
John Stuart Mill's *On Liberty*
Thomas Paine's *Common Sense*
Thomas Paine's *Rights of Man*
Geoffrey Parker's *Global Crisis: War, Climate Change and Catastrophe in the Seventeenth Century*
Jonathan Riley-Smith's *The First Crusade and the Idea of Crusading*
Jean-Jacques Rousseau's *The Social Contract*
Joan Wallach Scott's *Gender and the Politics of History*
Theda Skocpol's *States and Social Revolutions*
Adam Smith's *The Wealth of Nations*
Timothy Snyder's *Bloodlands: Europe Between Hitler and Stalin*
Sun Tzu's *The Art of War*
Keith Thomas's *Religion and the Decline of Magic*
Thucydides's *The History of the Peloponnesian War*
Frederick Jackson Turner's *The Significance of the Frontier in American History*
Odd Arne Westad's *The Global Cold War: Third World Interventions And The Making Of Our Times*

LITERATURE

Chinua Achebe's *An Image of Africa: Racism in Conrad's Heart of Darkness*
Roland Barthes's *Mythologies*
Homi K. Bhabha's *The Location of Culture*
Judith Butler's *Gender Trouble*
Simone De Beauvoir's *The Second Sex*
Ferdinand De Saussure's *Course in General Linguistics*
T. S. Eliot's *The Sacred Wood: Essays on Poetry and Criticism*
Zora Neale Huston's *Characteristics of Negro Expression*
Toni Morrison's *Playing in the Dark: Whiteness in the American Literary Imagination*
Edward Said's *Orientalism*
Gayatri Chakravorty Spivak's *Can the Subaltern Speak?*
Mary Wollstonecraft's *A Vindication of the Rights of Women*
Virginia Woolf's *A Room of One's Own*

PHILOSOPHY

Elizabeth Anscombe's *Modern Moral Philosophy*
Hannah Arendt's *The Human Condition*
Aristotle's *Metaphysics*
Aristotle's *Nicomachean Ethics*
Edmund Gettier's *Is Justified True Belief Knowledge?*
Georg Wilhelm Friedrich Hegel's *Phenomenology of Spirit*
David Hume's *Dialogues Concerning Natural Religion*
David Hume's *The Enquiry for Human Understanding*
Immanuel Kant's *Religion within the Boundaries of Mere Reason*
Immanuel Kant's *Critique of Pure Reason*
Søren Kierkegaard's *The Sickness Unto Death*
Søren Kierkegaard's *Fear and Trembling*
C. S. Lewis's *The Abolition of Man*
Alasdair MacIntyre's *After Virtue*
Marcus Aurelius's *Meditations*
Friedrich Nietzsche's *On the Genealogy of Morality*
Friedrich Nietzsche's *Beyond Good and Evil*
Plato's *Republic*
Plato's *Symposium*
Jean-Jacques Rousseau's *The Social Contract*
Gilbert Ryle's *The Concept of Mind*
Baruch Spinoza's *Ethics*
Sun Tzu's *The Art of War*
Ludwig Wittgenstein's *Philosophical Investigations*

POLITICS

Benedict Anderson's *Imagined Communities*
Aristotle's *Politics*
Bernard Bailyn's *The Ideological Origins of the American Revolution*
Edmund Burke's *Reflections on the Revolution in France*
John C. Calhoun's *A Disquisition on Government*
Ha-Joon Chang's *Kicking Away the Ladder*
Hamid Dabashi's *Iran: A People Interrupted*
Hamid Dabashi's *Theology of Discontent: The Ideological Foundation of the Islamic Revolution in Iran*
Robert Dahl's *Democracy and its Critics*
Robert Dahl's *Who Governs?*
David Brion Davis's *The Problem of Slavery in the Age of Revolution*

Alexis De Tocqueville's *Democracy in America*
James Ferguson's *The Anti-Politics Machine*
Frank Dikotter's *Mao's Great Famine*
Sheila Fitzpatrick's *Everyday Stalinism*
Eric Foner's *Reconstruction: America's Unfinished Revolution, 1863-1877*
Milton Friedman's *Capitalism and Freedom*
Francis Fukuyama's *The End of History and the Last Man*
John Lewis Gaddis's *We Now Know: Rethinking Cold War History*
Ernest Gellner's *Nations and Nationalism*
David Graeber's *Debt: the First 5000 Years*
Antonio Gramsci's *The Prison Notebooks*
Alexander Hamilton, John Jay & James Madison's *The Federalist Papers*
Friedrich Hayek's *The Road to Serfdom*
Christopher Hill's *The World Turned Upside Down*
Thomas Hobbes's *Leviathan*
John A. Hobson's *Imperialism: A Study*
Samuel P. Huntington's *The Clash of Civilizations and the Remaking of World Order*
Tony Judt's *Postwar: A History of Europe Since 1945*
David C. Kang's *China Rising: Peace, Power and Order in East Asia*
Paul Kennedy's *The Rise and Fall of Great Powers*
Robert Keohane's *After Hegemony*
Martin Luther King Jr.'s *Why We Can't Wait*
Henry Kissinger's *World Order: Reflections on the Character of Nations and the Course of History*
John Locke's *Two Treatises of Government*
Niccolò Machiavelli's *The Prince*
Thomas Robert Malthus's *An Essay on the Principle of Population*
Mahmood Mamdani's *Citizen and Subject: Contemporary Africa And The Legacy Of Late Colonialism*
Karl Marx's *Capital*
John Stuart Mill's *On Liberty*
John Stuart Mill's *Utilitarianism*
Hans Morgenthau's *Politics Among Nations*
Thomas Paine's *Common Sense*
Thomas Paine's *Rights of Man*
Thomas Piketty's *Capital in the Twenty-First Century*
Robert D. Putman's *Bowling Alone*
John Rawls's *Theory of Justice*
Jean-Jacques Rousseau's *The Social Contract*
Theda Skocpol's *States and Social Revolutions*
Adam Smith's *The Wealth of Nations*
Sun Tzu's *The Art of War*
Henry David Thoreau's *Civil Disobedience*
Thucydides's *The History of the Peloponnesian War*
Kenneth Waltz's *Theory of International Politics*
Max Weber's *Politics as a Vocation*
Odd Arne Westad's *The Global Cold War: Third World Interventions And The Making Of Our Times*

POSTCOLONIAL STUDIES

Roland Barthes's *Mythologies*
Frantz Fanon's *Black Skin, White Masks*
Homi K. Bhabha's *The Location of Culture*
Gustavo Gutiérrez's *A Theology of Liberation*
Edward Said's *Orientalism*
Gayatri Chakravorty Spivak's *Can the Subaltern Speak?*

PSYCHOLOGY

Gordon Allport's *The Nature of Prejudice*
Alan Baddeley & Graham Hitch's *Aggression: A Social Learning Analysis*
Albert Bandura's *Aggression: A Social Learning Analysis*
Leon Festinger's *A Theory of Cognitive Dissonance*
Sigmund Freud's *The Interpretation of Dreams*
Betty Friedan's *The Feminine Mystique*
Michael R. Gottfredson & Travis Hirschi's *A General Theory of Crime*
Eric Hoffer's *The True Believer: Thoughts on the Nature of Mass Movements*
William James's *Principles of Psychology*
Elizabeth Loftus's *Eyewitness Testimony*
A. H. Maslow's *A Theory of Human Motivation*
Stanley Milgram's *Obedience to Authority*
Steven Pinker's *The Better Angels of Our Nature*
Oliver Sacks's *The Man Who Mistook His Wife For a Hat*
Richard Thaler & Cass Sunstein's *Nudge: Improving Decisions About Health, Wealth and Happiness*
Amos Tversky's *Judgment under Uncertainty: Heuristics and Biases*
Philip Zimbardo's *The Lucifer Effect*

SCIENCE

Rachel Carson's *Silent Spring*
William Cronon's *Nature's Metropolis: Chicago And The Great West*
Alfred W. Crosby's *The Columbian Exchange*
Charles Darwin's *On the Origin of Species*
Richard Dawkin's *The Selfish Gene*
Thomas Kuhn's *The Structure of Scientific Revolutions*
Geoffrey Parker's *Global Crisis: War, Climate Change and Catastrophe in the Seventeenth Century*
Mathis Wackernagel & William Rees's *Our Ecological Footprint*

SOCIOLOGY

Michelle Alexander's *The New Jim Crow: Mass Incarceration in the Age of Colorblindness*
Gordon Allport's *The Nature of Prejudice*
Albert Bandura's *Aggression: A Social Learning Analysis*
Hanna Batatu's *The Old Social Classes And The Revolutionary Movements Of Iraq*
Ha-Joon Chang's *Kicking Away the Ladder*
W. E. B. Du Bois's *The Souls of Black Folk*
Émile Durkheim's *On Suicide*
Frantz Fanon's *Black Skin, White Masks*
Frantz Fanon's *The Wretched of the Earth*
Eric Foner's *Reconstruction: America's Unfinished Revolution, 1863-1877*
Eugene Genovese's *Roll, Jordan, Roll: The World the Slaves Made*
Jack Goldstone's *Revolution and Rebellion in the Early Modern World*
Antonio Gramsci's *The Prison Notebooks*
Richard Herrnstein & Charles A Murray's *The Bell Curve: Intelligence and Class Structure in American Life*
Eric Hoffer's *The True Believer: Thoughts on the Nature of Mass Movements*
Jane Jacobs's *The Death and Life of Great American Cities*
Robert Lucas's *Why Doesn't Capital Flow from Rich to Poor Countries?*
Jay Macleod's *Ain't No Makin' It: Aspirations and Attainment in a Low Income Neighborhood*
Elaine May's *Homeward Bound: American Families in the Cold War Era*
Douglas McGregor's *The Human Side of Enterprise*
C. Wright Mills's *The Sociological Imagination*

Thomas Piketty's *Capital in the Twenty-First Century*
Robert D. Putman's *Bowling Alone*
David Riesman's *The Lonely Crowd: A Study of the Changing American Character*
Edward Said's *Orientalism*
Joan Wallach Scott's *Gender and the Politics of History*
Theda Skocpol's *States and Social Revolutions*
Max Weber's *The Protestant Ethic and the Spirit of Capitalism*

THEOLOGY

Augustine's *Confessions*
Benedict's *Rule of St Benedict*
Gustavo Gutiérrez's *A Theology of Liberation*
Carole Hillenbrand's *The Crusades: Islamic Perspectives*
David Hume's *Dialogues Concerning Natural Religion*
Immanuel Kant's *Religion within the Boundaries of Mere Reason*
Ernst Kantorowicz's *The King's Two Bodies: A Study in Medieval Political Theology*
Søren Kierkegaard's *The Sickness Unto Death*
C. S. Lewis's *The Abolition of Man*
Saba Mahmood's *The Politics of Piety: The Islamic Revival and the Feminist Subject*
Baruch Spinoza's *Ethics*
Keith Thomas's *Religion and the Decline of Magic*

Macat Disciplines

Access the greatest ideas and thinkers across entire disciplines, including

AFRICANA STUDIES

Chinua Achebe's *An Image of Africa: Racism in Conrad's Heart of Darkness*

W. E. B. Du Bois's *The Souls of Black Folk*

Zora Neale Hurston's *Characteristics of Negro Expression*

Martin Luther King Jr.'s *Why We Can't Wait*

Toni Morrison's *Playing in the Dark: Whiteness in the American Literary Imagination*

Macat analyses are available from all good bookshops and libraries.

Access hundreds of analyses through one, multimedia tool.
Join free for one month **library.macat.com**

Macat Disciplines

Access the greatest ideas and thinkers across entire disciplines, including

FEMINISM, GENDER AND QUEER STUDIES

Simone De Beauvoir's
The Second Sex

Michel Foucault's
History of Sexuality

Betty Friedan's
The Feminine Mystique

Saba Mahmood's
*The Politics of Piety:
The Islamic Revival and
the Feminist Subject*

Joan Wallach Scott's
*Gender and the
Politics of History*

Mary Wollstonecraft's
*A Vindication of the
Rights of Woman*

Virginia Woolf's
A Room of One's Own

Judith Butler's
Gender Trouble

Macat analyses are available from all good bookshops and libraries.

Access hundreds of analyses through one, multimedia tool.
Join free for one month **library.macat.com**

Macat Disciplines

Access the greatest ideas and thinkers across entire disciplines, including

INEQUALITY

Ha-Joon Chang's, *Kicking Away the Ladder*
David Graeber's, *Debt: The First 5000 Years*
Robert E. Lucas's, *Why Doesn't Capital Flow from Rich To Poor Countries?*
Thomas Piketty's, *Capital in the Twenty-First Century*
Amartya Sen's, *Inequality Re-Examined*
Mahbub Ul Haq's, *Reflections on Human Development*

Macat Disciplines

Access the greatest ideas and thinkers across entire disciplines, including

CRIMINOLOGY

Michelle Alexander's
The New Jim Crow: Mass Incarceration in the Age of Colorblindness

Michael R. Gottfredson & Travis Hirschi's
A General Theory of Crime

Elizabeth Loftus's
Eyewitness Testimony

Richard Herrnstein & Charles A. Murray's
The Bell Curve: Intelligence and Class Structure in American Life

Jay Macleod's
Ain't No Makin' It: Aspirations and Attainment in a Low-Income Neighborhood

Philip Zimbardo's
The Lucifer Effect